GREAT JOBS

FOR

Economics Majors

Blythe Camenson

McGraw Hill

New York Chicago San Francisco Lisbon London Madrid Mexico City
Milan New Delhi San Juan Seoul Singapore Sydney Toronto

Library of Congress Cataloging-in-Publication Data

Camenson, Blythe.
    Great jobs for economics majors / by Blythe Camenson. — 2nd ed.
        p.   cm
    Contents: Pt. 1. The job search — pt. 2. The career paths.
    ISBN 0-07-146774-2 (pbk. alk.)
    1. Vocational guidance—United States.   I. Title.

  HF5382.5.U5C25196   2006
  330.023'73—dc22   2006044867

1 2 3 4 5 6 7 8 9 10 11 12 13 14 15 16 17 18 19 20 21   DOC/DOC   0 9 8 7 6

ISBN-13: 978-0-07-146774-2
ISBN-10:   0-07-146774-2

McGraw-Hill books are available at special quantity discounts to use as premiums and sales promotions, or for use in corporate training programs. For more information, please write to the Director of Special Sales, Professional Publishing, McGraw-Hill, Two Penn Plaza, New York, NY 10121-2298. Or contact your local bookstore.

This book is printed on acid-free paper.

Contents

Acknowledgments

The author would like to thank the following professionals for providing information and advice on careers for economics majors:

Robyn Bramhall, human resources
Chris Fuller, marketing and sales
Richard G. Leader, institutional sales
J. Douglas Nobles, loan officer/president
Jim Van Laningham, U.S. Foreign Service

The editors would like to thank Brad Crawford for preparing this edition.

Introduction

Economics: The New New Thing

This isn't your father's econ. Somewhere between Alan Greenspan's masterful tango with the go-go '90s market and the publication of Steven Levitt and Stephen Dubner's *Freakonomics,* the once dismal science became almost cool. More than that, it has become one of the hottest and most in-demand college majors around. Employers like graduates' critical thinking abilities, rapid adjustment to change, and grasp of the big picture. Job seekers like the degree's utility and high starting salaries.

More than 16,000 economics majors graduated from U.S. colleges and universities in the 2003–2004 school year, roughly a 40 percent increase from five years before. At many of the country's most prestigious universities, the gains were even higher. And the increase isn't limited to North America alone. From Europe to Asia, the major's popularity is surging.

The trend has corresponded to the rise of the Information Age and globalization. Economics provides the tools to dissect the new wealth of data available and make smart business decisions that will have far-reaching effects, and companies are willing pay people who have the tools. According to a 2005 survey by the National Association of Colleges and Employers, economics majors received average offers of $41,994 out of college. Though this puts economics solidly below such majors as chemical engineering and computer science, the average starting salary ranks above most business majors and nearly all liberal arts majors. Very cool, indeed.

What Is Economics?

Economics is the study of the way society uses its limited resources to produce the goods and services that it needs. It is a social science that studies many of the problems facing our society, and it is the foundation of most theories of business finance, management, and marketing.

Economics provides a logical, ordered way of looking at various problems. Whether we are discussing how a firm decides where to locate a business, how individuals choose where to invest their money, or how the federal government determines how to balance the budget, each is faced with the problem of making a decision about the best use of limited resources. Economics provides a logical method of analyzing the trade-offs involved in the decision-making process.

There are many fields within economics. Microeconomics is the study of smaller units of the economy, such as firms and households, and is often concerned with issues such as competition, markets, prices, incomes, and efficiency. Macroeconomics is the study of the aggregate economy. It focuses on inflation, unemployment, interest rates, economic growth, taxation, international trade, and international financial flows. Other areas of economics specialization include labor issues, urban topics, international economics, economic development, comparative economic systems, money and banking, health care, public finance, law and economics, transportation, the gaming industry, natural resource economics, common markets, econometrics, and mathematical economics.

Making Sense of It All

Economics is a powerful tool that helps you understand the world better. It is the foundation of all business studies. Economics majors have a good deal of institutional knowledge about the business world, the economic environment in which businesses operate, and the government policies that affect businesses. Further, economics majors are viewed as having developed their ability to analyze and communicate the results of their analysis.

A major in economics is attractive to job recruiters and graduate school admissions directors because of the excellent background it provides in critical thinking and quantitative analysis.

Where Can I Work?

Jobs held by economists are spread throughout many occupations. A major in economics prepares you for a wide range of professional careers.

Managerial training programs in many firms, including banks, other financial institutions, and large manufacturing companies, are open to economics majors. Economists are employed by businesses to study market problems, make predictions concerning market trends, and analyze how the overall economic system will affect a particular industry.

There are many opportunities for economics-related employment in government at the local, state, and federal levels. Economists working in government analyze public policy issues such as taxation, labor markets, welfare, international trade, and transportation. Research and consulting firms also employ economists in such areas as forecasting and industry analysis. Academic economists teach and do research on a variety of theoretical and applied topics. An undergraduate degree in economics provides excellent preparation for graduate programs in law, business, and social sciences including economics. In Chapters 5 through 10, you'll learn more details about these and many other career paths.

PART ONE

THE JOB SEARCH

The Self-Assessment

Self-assessment is the process by which you begin to acknowledge your own particular blend of education, experiences, values, needs, and goals. It provides the foundation for career planning and the entire job search process. Self-assessment involves looking inward and asking yourself what can sometimes prove to be difficult questions. This self-examination should lead to an intimate understanding of your personal traits and values, consumption patterns and economic needs, longer-term goals, skill base, preferred skills, and underdeveloped skills.

You come to the self-assessment process knowing yourself well in some of these areas, but you may still be uncertain about other aspects. You may be well aware of your consumption patterns, but have you spent much time specifically identifying your longer-term goals or your personal values as they relate to work? No matter what level of self-assessment you have undertaken to date, it is now time to clarify all of these issues and questions as they relate to the job search.

The knowledge you gain in the self-assessment process will guide the rest of your job search. In this book, you will learn about all of the following tasks:

- Writing résumés and cover letters
- Researching careers and networking
- Interviewing and job offer considerations

In each of these steps, you will rely on and often return to the understanding gained through your self-assessment. Any individual seeking employment must be able and willing to express these facets of his or her personality to recruiters and interviewers throughout the job search. This communication allows you to show the world who you are so that together with employers you can determine whether there will be a workable match with a given job or career path.

How to Conduct a Self-Assessment

The self-assessment process goes on naturally all the time. People ask you to clarify what you mean, you make a purchasing decision, or you begin a new relationship. You react to the world and the world reacts to you. How you understand these interactions and any changes you might make because of them are part of the natural process of self-discovery. There is, however, a more comprehensive and efficient way to approach self-assessment with regard to employment.

Because self-assessment can become a complex exercise, we have distilled it into a seven-step process that provides an effective basis for undertaking a job search. The seven steps include the following:

1. Understanding your personal traits
2. Identifying your personal values
3. Calculating your economic needs
4. Exploring your longer-term goals
5. Enumerating your skill base
6. Recognizing your preferred skills
7. Assessing skills needing further development

As you work through your self-assessment, you might want to create a worksheet similar to the one shown in Exhibit 1.1, starting on the following page. Or you might want to keep a journal of the thoughts you have as you undergo this process. There will be many opportunities to revise your self-assessment as you start down the path of seeking a career.

Step 1   Understand Your Personal Traits
Each person has a unique personality that he or she brings to the job search process. Gaining a better understanding of your personal traits can help you evaluate job and career choices. Identifying these traits and then finding employment that allows you to draw on at least some of them can create a rewarding and fulfilling work experience. If potential employment doesn't allow you to use these preferred traits, it is important to decide whether you

Exhibit 1.1
SELF-ASSESSMENT WORKSHEET

Step 1. Understand Your Personal Traits

The personal traits that describe me are
(Include all of the words that describe you.)
The ten personal traits that most accurately describe me are
(List these ten traits.)

Step 2. Identify Your Personal Values

Working conditions that are important to me include
(List working conditions that would have to exist for you to accept a position.)
The values that go along with my working conditions are
(Write down the values that correspond to each working condition.)
Some additional values I've decided to include are
(List those values you identify as you conduct this job search.)

Step 3. Calculate Your Economic Needs

My estimated minimum annual salary requirement is
(Write the salary you have calculated based on your budget.)
Starting salaries for the positions I'm considering are
(List the name of each job you are considering and the associated starting salary.)

Step 4. Explore Your Longer-Term Goals

My thoughts on longer-term goals right now are
(Jot down some of your longer-term goals as you know them right now.)

Step 5. Enumerate Your Skill Base

The general skills I possess are
(List the skills that underlie tasks you are able to complete.)
The specific skills I possess are
(List more technical or specific skills that you possess, and indicate your level of expertise.)
General and specific skills that I want to promote to employers for the jobs I'm considering are
(List general and specific skills for each type of job you are considering.)

continued

Step 6. Recognize Your Preferred Skills

Skills that I would like to use on the job include

(List skills that you hope to use on the job, and indicate how often you'd like to use them.)

Step 7. Assess Skills Needing Further Development

Some skills that I'll need to acquire for the jobs I'm considering include

(Write down skills listed in job advertisements or job descriptions that you don't currently possess.)

I believe I can build these skills by

(Describe how you plan to acquire these skills.)

can find other ways to express them or whether you would be better off not considering this type of job. Interests and hobbies pursued outside of work hours can be one way to use personal traits you don't have an opportunity to draw on in your work. For example, if you consider yourself an outgoing person and the kinds of jobs you are examining allow little contact with other people, you may be able to achieve the level of interaction that is comfortable for you outside of your work setting. If such a compromise seems impractical or otherwise unsatisfactory, you probably should explore only jobs that provide the interaction you want and need on the job.

Many young adults who are not very confident about their employability will downplay their need for income. They will say, "Money is not all that important if I love my work." But if you begin to document exactly what you need for housing, transportation, insurance, clothing, food, and utilities, you will begin to understand that some jobs cannot meet your financial needs and it doesn't matter how wonderful the job is. If you have to worry each payday about bills and other financial obligations, you won't be very effective on the job. Begin now to be honest with yourself about your needs.

Begin the self-assessment process by creating an inventory of your personal traits. Make a list of as many words as possible to describe yourself. Words like *accurate, creative, future-oriented, relaxed,* or *structured* are just a few examples. In addition, you might ask people who know you well how they might describe you.

Focus on Selected Personal Traits. Of all the traits you identified, select the ten you believe most accurately describe you. Keep track of these ten traits.

Consider Your Personal Traits in the Job Search Process. As you begin exploring jobs and careers, watch for matches between your personal traits and the job descriptions you read. Some jobs will require many personal traits you know you possess, and others will not seem to match those traits.

For example, economists doing traditional market analysis often have head-down, data-driven jobs that require independent work and a degree of isolation, which is common in many positions in the profession. Gregarious individuals who prefer a lot of social interaction and overt incentives for performance might be better suited to sales, where interpersonal skills are paramount. Both types of positions require solid communications skills and intrinsic motivation, but in different ways.

Your ability to respond to changing conditions, your decision-making ability, productivity, creativity, and verbal skills all have a bearing on your success in and enjoyment of your work life. To better guarantee success, be sure to take the time needed to understand these traits in yourself.

Step 2   Identify Your Personal Values

Your personal values affect every aspect of your life, including employment, and they develop and change as you move through life. Values can be defined as principles that we hold in high regard, qualities that are important and desirable to us. Some values aren't ordinarily connected to work (love, beauty, color, light, relationships, family, or religion), and others are (autonomy, cooperation, effectiveness, achievement, knowledge, and security). Our values determine, in part, the level of satisfaction we feel in a particular job.

Define Acceptable Working Conditions. One facet of employment is the set of working conditions that must exist for someone to consider taking a job.

Each of us would probably create a unique list of acceptable working conditions, but items that might be included on many people's lists are the amount of money you would need to be paid, how far you are willing to drive or travel, the amount of freedom you want in determining your own schedule, whether you would be working with people or data or things, and the types of tasks you would be willing to do. Your conditions might include statements of working conditions you will *not* accept; for example, you might not be willing to work at night or on weekends or holidays.

If you were offered a job tomorrow, what conditions would have to exist for you to realistically consider accepting the position? Take some time and make a list of these conditions.

Realize Associated Values. Your list of working conditions can be used to create an inventory of your values relating to jobs and careers you are exploring. For example, if one of your conditions stated that you wanted to earn at least $30,000 per year, the associated value would be financial gain. If another condition was that you wanted to work with a friendly group of people, the value that went along with that might be belonging or interaction with people.

Relate Your Values to the World of Work. As you read the job descriptions you come across either in this book, in newspapers and magazines, or online, think about the values associated with each position.

Economists work in a wide variety of fields. Knowing what makes the work important to you will help you choose the right type of job. Are you goal-oriented? A job as a trader or broker might be right for you. Relationship-oriented? Perhaps teaching or human resources is where you belong. Most jobs combine elements of both. For example, loan officers are expected to write so much business per day, but they also need to empathize with customers and develop solutions compatible with their personal circumstances.

At least some of the associated values in the field you're exploring should match those you extracted from your list of working conditions. Take a second look at any values that don't match up. How important are they to you? What will happen if they are not satisfied on the job? Can you incorporate those personal values elsewhere? Your answers need to be brutally honest. As you continue your exploration, be sure to add to your list any additional values that occur to you.

Step 3   Calculate Your Economic Needs

Each of us grew up in an environment that provided for certain basic needs, such as food and shelter, and, to varying degrees, other needs that we now consider basic, such as cable television, e-mail, or an automobile. Needs such as privacy, space, and quiet, which at first glance may not appear to be monetary needs, may add to housing expenses and so should be considered as you examine your economic needs. For example, if you place a high value on a large, open living space for yourself, it would be difficult to satisfy that need without an associated high housing cost, especially in a densely populated city environment.

As you prepare to move into the world of work and become responsible for meeting your own basic needs, it is important to consider the salary you will need to be able to afford a satisfying standard of living. The three-step process outlined here will help you plan a budget, which in turn will allow you to evaluate the various career choices and geographic locations you are considering. The steps include (1) develop a realistic budget, (2) examine starting salaries, and (3) use a cost-of-living index.

Develop a Realistic Budget. Each of us has certain expectations for the kind of lifestyle we want to maintain. To begin the process of defining your economic needs, it will be helpful to determine what you expect to spend on routine monthly expenses. These expenses include housing, food, transportation, entertainment, utilities, loan repayments, and revolving charge accounts. You may not currently spend anything for certain items, but you probably will have to once you begin supporting yourself. As you develop this budget, be generous in your estimates, but keep in mind any items that could be reduced or eliminated. If you are not sure about the cost of a certain item, talk with family or friends who would be able to give you a realistic estimate.

If this is new or difficult for you, start to keep a log of expenses right now. You may be surprised at how much you actually spend each month for food or stamps or magazines. Household expenses and personal grooming items can often loom very large in a budget, as can auto repairs or home maintenance.

Income taxes must also be taken into consideration when examining salary requirements. State and local taxes vary, so it is difficult to calculate exactly the effect of taxes on the amount of income you need to generate. To roughly estimate the gross income necessary to generate your minimum annual salary requirement, multiply the minimum salary you have calculated by a factor of 1.35. The resulting figure will be an approximation of what your gross income would need to be, given your estimated expenses.

Examine Starting Salaries. Starting salaries for each of the career tracks are provided throughout this book. These salary figures can be used in conjunction with the cost-of-living index (discussed in the next section) to determine whether you would be able to meet your basic economic needs in a given geographic location.

Use a Cost-of-Living Index. If you are thinking about trying to get a job in a geographic region other than the one where you now live, understanding differences in the cost of living will help you come to a more informed decision about making a move. By using a cost-of-living index, you can compare salaries offered and the cost of living in different locations with what you know about the salaries offered and the cost of living in your present location.

Many variables are used to calculate the cost-of-living index. Often included are housing, groceries, utilities, transportation, health care, clothing, and entertainment expenses. Right now you do not need to worry about the details associated with calculating a given index. The main purpose of this exercise is to help you understand that pay ranges for entry-level positions may not vary greatly, but the cost of living in different locations *can* vary tremendously.

Websites such as Salary.com (http://swz.salary.com/CostOfLiving Wizard/layoutscripts/coll_start.asp) and Homestore.com (home store.com/move/tools/salarycalc.asp) have salary calculators that will compare the cost of living in different parts of the country to help you figure out how much you need to make. Locations are broken down into cities and in some cases, as in New York City and Southern California, subregions of metro areas to accurately reflect your expenses.

These comparisons are based on a cost-of-living index that takes into account the prices for housing, utilities, and consumer goods in a given area and assigns it a value relative to other areas. An index of 100 is the average for all areas considered. Manhattan's index is substantially higher than 100; rural Mississippi's is much lower. Here's how it would work out for a worker in Charlotte, North Carolina, making $48,000 a year who's considering a move:

City	Income	
Charlotte, N.C.	$48,000	
New Locations	**Equivalent Salary**	**% Difference**
Greenville, MS.	$37,873	−21.1%
Orange County, Calif.	$59,391	23.7%

> Based on the cost-of-living difference, a worker moving from Charlotte to Greenville needs to earn only $37,873 in Greenville in order to maintain his/her previous standard of living. Maintaining his/her present salary there would be equivalent to receiving a 21 percent raise. In Orange County, he/she would need to earn nearly $60,000 to match his/her previous income, and in St. Louis $44,000.

You can work through a similar exercise for any type of job you are considering and for many locations when current salary information is available. It will be worth your time to undertake this analysis if you are seriously considering a relocation. By doing so you will be able to make an informed choice.

Step 4   Explore Your Longer-Term Goals

There is no question that when we first begin working, our goals are to use our skills and education in a job that will reward us with employment, income, and status relative to the preparation we brought with us to this position. If we are not being paid as much as we feel we should for our level of education or if job demands don't provide the intellectual stimulation we had hoped for, we experience unhappiness and as a result often seek other employment.

Most jobs we consider "good" are those that fulfill our basic "lower-level" needs of security, food, clothing, shelter, income, and productive work. But even when our basic needs are met and our jobs are secure and productive, we as individuals are constantly changing. As we change, the demands and expectations we place on our jobs may change. Fortunately, some jobs grow and change with us, and this explains why some people are happy throughout many years in a job.

But more often people are bigger than the jobs they fill. We have more goals and needs than any job could satisfy. These are "higher-level" needs of self-esteem, companionship, affection, and an increasing desire to feel we are employing ourselves in the most effective way possible. Not all of these higher-level needs can be met through employment, but for as long as we are employed, we increasingly demand that our jobs play their part in moving us along the path to fulfillment.

Another obvious but important fact is that we change as we mature. Although our jobs also have the potential for change, they may not change as frequently or as markedly as we do. There are increasingly fewer one-job, one-employer careers; we must think about a work future that may involve voluntary or forced moves from employer to employer. Because of that very real possibility, we need to take advantage of the opportunities in each position we hold. Acquiring the skills and competencies associated with each position will keep us viable and attractive as employees. This is particularly true in a job market that not only is technology/computer dependent, but also is populated with more and more small, self-transforming organizations rather than the large, seemingly stable organizations of the past.

This holds true in economics too, although the rate of change and level of stability are drastically different depending on your career path. Jobs in teaching and government tend to be highly stabile and offer predictable opportunities for advancement. An economist working for a consulting firm could expect a more volatile path, one subject to the vagaries of market forces and new technologies. Especially in the latter case, it's helpful to talk to people in the field at several different levels—a consultant just a few years removed from school, one in mid-career, and the leader of a firm, for example—to gauge how the work has changed and consider where it's headed. Each will have a different perspective, unique concerns, and an individual set of priorities.

Step 5   Enumerate Your Skill Base

In terms of the job search, skills can be thought of as capabilities that can be developed in school, at work, or by volunteering and then used in specific job settings. Many studies have documented the kinds of skills that employers seek in entry-level applicants. For example, some of the most desired skills for individuals interested in the teaching profession are the ability to interact effectively with students one-on-one, to manage a classroom, to adapt to varying situations as necessary, and to get involved in school activities. Business employers have also identified important qualities, including enthusiasm for the employer's product or service, a businesslike mind, the ability to follow written or oral instructions, the ability to demonstrate self-control, the confidence to suggest new ideas, the ability to communicate with all members of a group, an awareness of cultural differences, and loyalty, to name just a few. You will find that many of these skills are also in the repertoire of qualities demanded in your college major.

To be successful in obtaining any given job, you must be able to demonstrate that you possess a certain mix of skills that will allow you to carry out the duties required by that job. This skill mix will vary a great deal from job to job; to determine the skills necessary for the jobs you are seeking, you can read job advertisements or more generic job descriptions, such as those found later in this book. If you want to be effective in the job search, you must directly show employers that you possess the skills needed to be successful in filling the position. These skills will initially be described on your résumé and then discussed again during the interview process.

Skills are either general or specific. To develop a list of skills relevant to employers, you must first identify the general skills you possess, then list specific skills you have to offer, and, finally, examine which of these skills employers are seeking.

Identify Your General Skills. Because you possess or will possess a college degree, employers will assume that you can read and write, perform certain basic computations, think critically, and communicate effectively. Employers will want to see that you have acquired these skills, and they will want to know which additional general skills you possess.

One way to begin identifying skills is to write an experiential diary. An experiential diary lists all the tasks you were responsible for completing for each job you've held and then outlines the skills required to do those tasks. You may list several skills for any given task. This diary allows you to distinguish between the tasks you performed and the underlying skills required to complete those tasks. Here's an example:

Tasks	Skills
Answering telephone	Effective use of language, clear diction, ability to direct inquiries, ability to solve problems
Waiting on tables	Poise under conditions of time and pressure, speed, accuracy, good memory, simultaneous completion of tasks, sales skills

For each job or experience you have participated in, develop a worksheet based on the example shown here. On a résumé, you may want to describe these skills rather than simply listing tasks. Skills are easier for the employer to appreciate, especially when your experience is very different from the employment you are seeking. In addition to helping you identify general skills, this experiential diary will prepare you to speak more effectively in an interview about the qualifications you possess.

Identify Your Specific Skills. It may be easier to identify your specific skills because you can definitely say whether you can speak other languages, program a computer, draft a map or diagram, or edit a document using appropriate symbols and terminology.

Using your experiential diary, identify the points in your history where you learned how to do something very specific, and decide whether you have a beginning, intermediate, or advanced knowledge of how to use that particular skill. Right now, be sure to list *every* specific skill you have, and don't consider whether you like using the skill. Write down a list of specific skills you have acquired and the level of competence you possess—beginning, intermediate, or advanced.

Relate Your Skills to Employers. You probably have thought about a couple of different jobs you might be interested in obtaining, and one way to begin relating the general and specific skills you possess to a potential employer's needs is to read actual advertisements for these types of positions (see Part Two for resources listing actual job openings).

For example, you might be interested in a career as a human resources recruiter. A typical job listing might read, "Candidates should have a bachelor's in HR or related field, up to one year of recruiting experience, strong written and verbal presentation skills, and the ability to manage competing priorities, often with compressed deadlines." Start deciding how your general traits and skills apply to the jobs you're interested in.

You can begin by building a comprehensive list of required skills with the first job description you read. Exploring job postings for and descriptions of several types of related positions will reveal an important core of skills necessary for obtaining the type of work you're interested in. In building the list, include both general traits and specific skills.

For an HR recruiter, you could compile a list of your skills and job skills that might look like the following:

JOB: HUMAN RESOURCES RECRUITER

General Traits	Specific Skills
Outgoing, persuasive personality	Make good first impressions and find best candidates
Good communicator	Interview candidates, orient new employees
Highly organized	Schedule interviews, check references
Effective reader for content	Quickly screen for best applicants
Have firm convictions	Reliable decision making
Focused	Ability to meet deadlines

On a separate sheet of paper, try to generate a comprehensive list of required skills for at least one job you are considering. The list of general skills that you develop for a given career path will be valuable for any number of jobs you might apply for. Many of the specific skills will also be transferable to other positions. For example, being outgoing, persuasive, and a good communicator would be valued not only in recruiters but in corporate trainers as well.

Step 6   Recognize Your Preferred Skills

In the previous section you developed a comprehensive list of skills that relate to particular career paths that are of interest to you. You can now relate these to skills that you prefer to use. We all use a wide range of skills (some researchers say individuals have a repertoire of about five hundred skills), but we may not particularly be interested in using all of them in our work. There may be some skills that come to us more naturally or that we use successfully time and time again and that we want to continue to use; these are best described as our preferred skills. For this exercise use the list of skills that you created for the previous section, and decide which of them you are *most interested in using* in future work and how often you would like to use them. You might be interested in using some skills only occasionally, while others you would like to use more regularly. You probably also have skills that you hope you can use constantly.

As you examine job announcements, look for matches between this list of preferred skills and the qualifications described in the advertisements. These skills should be highlighted on your résumé and discussed in job interviews.

Step 7   Assess Skills Needing Further Development

Previously you compiled a list of general and specific skills required for given positions. You already possess some of these skills; those that remain to be developed are your underdeveloped skills.

If you are just beginning the job search, there may be gaps between the qualifications required for some of the jobs you're considering and the skills you possess. The thought of having to admit to and talk about these underdeveloped skills, especially in a job interview, is a frightening one. One way to put a healthy perspective on this subject is to target and relate your exploration of underdeveloped skills to the types of positions you are seeking. Recognizing these shortcomings and planning to overcome them with either on-the-job training or additional formal education can be a positive way to address the concept of underdeveloped skills.

On your worksheet or in your journal, make a list of up to five general or specific skills required for the positions you're interested in that you *don't currently possess*. For each item list an idea you have for specific action you could take to acquire that skill. Do some brainstorming to come up with possible actions. If you have a hard time generating ideas, talk to people currently working in this type of position, professionals in your college career services office, trusted friends, family members, or members of related professional associations.

In the chapter on interviewing, we will discuss in detail how to effectively address questions about underdeveloped skills. Generally speaking, though, employers want genuine answers to these types of questions. They want you to reveal "the real you," and they also want to see how you answer difficult questions. In taking the positive, targeted approach discussed previously, you show the employer that you are willing to continue to learn and that you have a plan for strengthening your job qualifications.

Use Your Self-Assessment

Exploring entry-level career options can be an exciting experience if you have good resources available and will take the time to use them. Can you effectively complete the following tasks?

1. Understand your personality traits and relate them to career choices
2. Define your personal values
3. Determine your economic needs
4. Explore longer-term goals
5. Understand your skill base

6. Recognize your preferred skills
7. Express a willingness to improve on your underdeveloped skills

If so, then you can more meaningfully participate in the job search process by writing a more effective résumé, finding job titles that represent work you are interested in doing, locating job sites that will provide the opportunity for you to use your strengths and skills, networking in an informed way, participating in focused interviews, getting the most out of follow-up contacts, and evaluating job offers to find those that create a good match between you and the employer. The remaining chapters in Part One guide you through these next steps in the job search process. For many job seekers, this process can take anywhere from three months to a year to implement. The time you will need to put into your job search will depend on the type of job you want and the geographic location where you'd like to work. Think of your effort as a job in itself, requiring you to set aside time each week to complete the needed work. Carefully undertaken efforts may reduce the time you need for your job search.

2

The Résumé and Cover Letter

The task of writing a résumé may seem overwhelming if you are unfamiliar with this type of document, but there are some easily understood techniques that can and should be used. This section was written to help you understand the purpose of the résumé, the different types of formats available, and how to write the sections that contain information traditionally found on a résumé. We will present examples and explanations that address questions frequently posed by people writing their first résumé or updating an old one.

Even within the formats and suggestions given, however, there are infinite variations. True, most follow one of the outlines suggested, but you should feel free to adjust the résumé to suit your needs and make it expressive of your life and experience.

Why Write a Résumé?

The purpose of a résumé is to convince an employer that you should be interviewed. Whether you're mailing, faxing, or e-mailing this document, you'll want to present enough information to show that you can make an immediate and valuable contribution to an organization. A résumé is not an in-depth historical or legal document; later in the job search process you may be asked to document your entire work history on an application form and attest to its validity. The résumé should, instead, highlight relevant information pertaining directly to the organization that will receive the document or to the type of position you are seeking.

We will discuss the chronological and digital résumés in detail here. Functional and targeted résumés, which are used much less often, are briefly discussed. The reasons for using one type of résumé over another and the typical format for each are addressed in the following sections.

The Chronological Résumé

The chronological résumé is the most common of the various résumé formats and therefore the format that employers are most used to receiving. This type of résumé is easy to read and understand because it details the chronological progression of jobs you have held. (See Exhibit 2.1.) It begins with your most recent employment and works back in time. If you have a solid work history or have experience that provided growth and development in your duties and responsibilities, a chronological résumé will highlight these achievements. The typical elements of a chronological résumé include the heading, a career objective, educational background, employment experience, activities, and references.

The Heading
The heading consists of your name, address, telephone number, and other means of contact. This may include a fax number, e-mail address, and your home-page address. If you are using a shared e-mail account or a parent's business fax, be sure to let others who use these systems know that you may receive important professional correspondence via these systems. You wouldn't want to miss a vital e-mail or fax! Likewise, if your résumé directs readers to a personal home page on the Web, be certain it's a professional personal home page designed to be viewed and appreciated by a prospective employer. This may mean making substantial changes in the home page you currently mount on the Web.

The Objective
Without a doubt the objective statement is the most challenging part of the résumé for most writers. Even for individuals who have decided on a career path, it can be difficult to encapsulate all they want to say in one or two brief sentences. For job seekers who are unfocused or unclear about their intentions, trying to write this section can inhibit the entire résumé writing process.

Keep the objective as short as possible and no longer than two short sentences.

Exhibit 2.1
CHRONOLOGICAL RÉSUMÉ

JASON ST. GEMME
12504 Guterson Blvd.
Indianapolis, IN 46261
(765) 555-4872
jsg@site.com

OBJECTIVE
Tenure-track position as an economics professor at a four-year college or university.

EDUCATION
Doctorate in Economics
Georgetown University
Washington, DC
December 2004

Master of Science in Economics
Syracuse University
Syracuse, New York
May 1999
3.45 GPA on a 4.0 scale

Bachelor of Arts in Political Science
Syracuse University
Syracuse, New York
May 1997
Graduated magna cum laude

RELATED COURSEWORK
Minor in philosophy	Finance
Computer science	Entertainment law

continued

EXPERIENCE

Visiting Fellow, specializing in international labor markets
Brookings Institution
Washington, DC
February 2005 to present

Government Specialist
Krahts & Mayem
New York City
June 2001 to August 2002

Instructor, Economics 117
Syracuse University
Syracuse, New York
September 2000 to May 2001

Teaching Assistant, Economics 114
Syracuse University
Syracuse, New York
September 1998 to May 2000

COMMUNITY SERVICE

Red Cross: campaign chair, fund-drive coordinator (one year); Syracuse Youth
Collaborative (student mentoring), two years

REFERENCES

Personal and professional references available upon request.

Choose one of the following types of objective statement:

1. *General Objective Statement*

- An entry-level educational programming coordinator position

2. *Position-Focused Objective*

- To obtain the position of conference coordinator at State College

3. Industry-Focused Objective

- To begin a career as a sales representative in the cruise line industry

4. Summary of Qualifications Statement

A master's and Ph.D. in economics coupled with three years' teaching experience and deep research at one of the nation's premier centers for public policy have prepared me to continue my research and share my learnings to date with the next generation of economics students.

Support Your Objective. A résumé that contains any one of these types of objective statements should then go on to demonstrate why you are qualified to get the position. Listing academic degrees can be one way to indicate qualifications. Another demonstration would be in the way previous experiences, both volunteer and paid, are described. Without this kind of documentation in the body of the résumé, the objective looks unsupported. Think of the résumé as telling a connected story about you. All the elements should work together to form a coherent picture that ideally should relate to your statement of objective.

Education

This section of your résumé should indicate the exact name of the degree you will receive or have received, spelled out completely with no abbreviations. The degree is generally listed after the objective, followed by the institution name and location, and then the month and year of graduation. This section could also include your academic minor, grade point average (GPA), and appearance on the Dean's List or President's List.

If you have enough space, you might want to include a section listing courses related to the field in which you are seeking work. The best use of a "related courses" section would be to list some course work that is not traditionally associated with the major. Perhaps you took several computer courses outside your degree that will be helpful and related to the job prospects you are entertaining. Several education section examples are shown here:

- Bachelor of Science in Economics; University of Texas-El Paso, May 2005; Minor in business
- Bachelor of Arts in Economics; University of Wisconsin, Madison, Wis., 2004
- Bachelor of Science, Economics; University of Pennsylvania, Philadelphia, PA.; Minor: History

An example of a format for a related courses section follows:

Related Courses

Computer science	Auditing
Finance	Market research
Hotel and restaurant management	

Experience

The experience section of your résumé should be the most substantial part and should take up most of the space on the page. Employers want to see what kind of work history you have. They will look at your range of experiences, longevity in jobs, and specific tasks you are able to complete. This section may also be called "work experience," "related experience," "employment history," or "employment." No matter what you call this section, some important points to remember are the following:

1. **Describe your duties** as they relate to the position you are seeking.
2. **Emphasize major responsibilities** and indicate increases in responsibility. Include all relevant employment experiences: summer, part-time, internships, cooperative education, or self-employment.
3. **Emphasize skills**, especially those that transfer from one situation to another. The fact that you coordinated a student organization, chaired meetings, supervised others, and managed a budget leads one to suspect that you could coordinate other things as well.
4. **Use descriptive job titles** that provide information about what you did. A "Student Intern" should be more specifically stated as, for example, "Magazine Operations Intern." "Volunteer" is also too general; a title such as "Peer Writing Tutor" would be more appropriate.
5. **Create word pictures** by using active verbs to start sentences. Describe *results* you have produced in the work you have done.

A limp description would say something such as the following: "My duties included helping with production, proofreading, and editing. I used a design and page layout program." An action statement would be stated as follows: "Coordinated and assisted in the creative marketing of brochures and seminar promotions, becoming proficient in Quark."

Remember, an accomplishment is simply a result, a final measurable product that people can relate to. A duty is not a result; it is an obligation—every job holder has duties. For an effective résumé, list as many results as you can. To make the most of the limited space you have and to give your description impact, carefully select appropriate and accurate descriptors.

Here are some traits that employers tell us they like to see:

- Teamwork
- Energy and motivation
- Learning and using new skills
- Versatility
- Critical thinking
- Understanding how profits are created
- Organizational acumen
- Communicating directly and clearly, in both writing and speaking
- Risk taking
- Willingness to admit mistakes
- High personal standards

Solutions to Frequently Encountered Problems

Repetitive Employment with the Same Employer
EMPLOYMENT: The Foot Locker, Portland, Oregon. Summer 2001, 2002, 2003. Initially employed in high school as salesclerk. Because of successful performance, asked to return next two summers at higher pay with added responsibility. Ranked as the #2 salesperson the first summer and #1 the next two summers. Assisted in arranging eye-catching retail displays; served as manager of other summer workers during owner's absence.

A Large Number of Jobs
EMPLOYMENT: Recent Hospitality Industry Experience: Affiliated with four upscale hotel/restaurant complexes (September 2001–February 2004), where I worked part- and full-time as a waiter, bartender, disc jockey, and bookkeeper to produce income for college.

Several Positions with the Same Employer

EMPLOYMENT: Coca-Cola Bottling Co., Burlington, Vermont, 2001–2004. In four years, I received three promotions, each with increased pay and responsibility.

Summer Sales Coordinator: Promoted to hire, train, and direct efforts of add-on staff of fifteen college-age route salespeople hired to meet summer peak demand for product.

Sales Administrator: Promoted to run home office sales desk, managing accounts and associated delivery schedules for professional sales force of ten people. Intensive phone work, daily interaction with all personnel, and strong knowledge of product line required.

Route Salesperson: Summer employment to travel and tourism industry sites that use Coke products. Met specific schedule demands, used good communication skills with wide variety of customers, and demonstrated strong selling skills. Named salesperson of the month for July and August of that year.

Questions Résumé Writers Often Ask

How Far Back Should I Go in Terms of Listing Past Jobs?

Usually, listing three or four jobs should suffice. If you did something back in high school that has a bearing on your future aspirations for employment, by all means list the job. As you progress through your college career, high school jobs will be replaced on the résumé by college employment.

Should I Differentiate Between Paid and Nonpaid Employment?

Most employers are not initially concerned about how much you were paid. They are eager to know how much responsibility you held in your past employment. There is no need to specify that your work was as a volunteer if you had significant responsibilities.

How Should I Represent My Accomplishments or Work-Related Responsibilities?

Succinctly, but fully. In other words, give the employer enough information to arouse curiosity but not so much detail that you leave nothing to the imagination. Besides, some jobs merit more lengthy explanations than others. Be sure to convey any information that can give an employer a better understanding of the depth of your involvement at work. Did you supervise others? How many? Did your efforts result in a more efficient operation? How much did you increase efficiency? Did you handle a budget? How much? Were you promoted in a short time? Did you work two jobs at once or fifteen hours per week after high school? Where appropriate, quantify.

Should the Work Section Always Follow the Education Section on the Résumé?

Always lead with your strengths. If your education closely relates to the employment you now seek, put this section after the objective. If your education does not closely relate but you have a surplus of good work experiences, consider reversing the order of your sections to lead with employment, followed by education.

How Should I Present My Activities, Honors, Awards, Professional Societies, and Affiliations?

This section of the résumé can add valuable information for an employer to consider if used correctly. The rule of thumb for information in this section is to include only those activities that are in some way relevant to the objective stated on your résumé. If you can draw a valid connection between your activities and your objective, include them; if not, leave them out.

Professional affiliations and honors should all be listed; especially important are those related to your job objective. Social clubs and activities need not be a part of your résumé unless you hold a significant office or you are looking for a position related to your membership. Be aware that most prospective employers' principal concerns are related to your employability, not your social life. If you have any, publications can be included as an addendum to your résumé.

How Should I Handle References?

The use of references is considered a part of the interview process, and they should never be listed on a résumé. You would always provide references to a potential employer if requested to, so it is not even necessary to include this section on the résumé if space does not permit. If space is available, it is acceptable to include the following statement:

- References furnished upon request.

The Functional Résumé

The functional résumé departs from a chronological résumé in that it organizes information by specific accomplishments in various settings: previous jobs, volunteer work, associations, and so forth. This type of résumé permits you to stress the substance of your experiences rather than the position titles you have held. You should consider using a functional résumé if you have held a series of similar jobs that relied on the same skills or abilities. There are many good books in which you can find examples of functional résumés, including *How to Write a Winning Resume* or *Resumes Made Easy*.

The Targeted Résumé

The targeted résumé focuses on specific work-related capabilities you can bring to a given position within an organization. Past achievements are listed to highlight your capabilities and the work history section is abbreviated.

Digital Résumés

Today's employers have to manage an enormous number of résumés. One of the most frequent complaints the writers of this series hear from students is the failure of employers to even acknowledge the receipt of a résumé and cover letter. Frequently, the reason for this poor response or nonresponse is the volume of applications received for every job. In an attempt to better manage the considerable labor investment involved in processing large numbers of résumés, many employers are requiring digital submission of résumés. There are two types of digital résumés: those that can be e-mailed or posted to a website, called *electronic résumés*, and those that can be "read" by a computer, commonly called *scannable résumés*. Though the format may be a bit different from the traditional "paper" résumé, the goal of both types of digital résumés is the same—to get you an interview! These résumés must be designed to be "technologically friendly." What that basically means to you is that they should be free of graphics and fancy formatting. (See Exhibit 2.2.)

Electronic Résumés

Sometimes referred to as plain-text résumés, electronic résumés are designed to be e-mailed to an employer or posted to one of many commercial Internet databases such as CareerMosaic.com, America's Job Bank (ajb.dni.us), or Monster.com.

Exhibit 2.2
DIGITAL RÉSUMÉ

JASON ST. GEMME
12504 Guterson Blvd.
Indianapolis, IN 46261
(765) 555-4872
jsg@site.com

Put your name at the top on its own line.

Put your phone number on its own line.

KEYWORD SUMMARY
Labor research
Brookings
Economic analysis
Government regulation
Teaching professional

Keywords make your résumé easier to find in a database.

Use a standard-width typeface.

EXPERIENCE
* Fellowship. February 2005 to present; Brookings
  Institution.
Visiting fellow specializing in international labor markets.
Published findings in academic and consumer
  publications.
* Agency. June 2001 to August 2002; Krahts & Mayem.
Government specialist; assessed effects of regulation on
  corporate markets.
* University. September 2000 to May 2001; Syracuse
  University. Instructor, Economics 117, "Principles of
  Microeconomics," freshmen and sophomores.
* University, September 1998 to May 2000; Syracuse
  University. Teaching Assistant, Economics 114, "Principles
  of Macroeconomics," freshmen and sophomores.

Use a space between asterisk and text.

No line should exceed sixty-five characters.

Capitalize letters to emphasize heading

COMMUNITY SERVICE
* Campaign chair, fund-drive coordinator, Red Cross.
* Student mentor, Syracuse Youth Collaborative.

End each line by hitting the ENTER (or RETURN) key.

Some technical considerations:

- Electronic résumés must be written in American Standard Code for Information Interchange (ASCII), which is simply a plain-text format. These characters are universally recognized so that every computer can accurately read and understand them. To create an ASCII file of your current résumé, open your document, then save it as a text or ASCII file. This will eliminate all formatting. Edit as needed using your computer's text editor application.
- Use a standard-width typeface. Courier is a good choice because it is the font associated with ASCII in most systems.
- Use a font size of 11 to 14 points. A 12-point font is considered standard.
- Your margin should be left-justified.
- Do not exceed sixty-five characters per line because the word-wrap function doesn't operate in ASCII.
- Do not use boldface, italics, underlining, bullets, or various font sizes. Instead, use asterisks, plus signs, or all capital letters when you want to emphasize something.
- Avoid graphics and shading.
- Use as many "keywords" as you possibly can. These are words or phrases usually relating to skills or experience that either are specifically used in the job announcement or are popular buzzwords in the industry.
- Minimize abbreviations.
- Your name should be the first line of text.
- Conduct a "test run" by e-mailing your résumé to yourself and a friend before you send it to the employer. See how it transmits, and make any changes you need to. Continue to test it until it's exactly how you want it to look.
- Unless an employer specifically requests that you send the résumé in the form of an attachment, don't. Employers can encounter problems opening a document as an attachment, and there are always viruses to consider.
- Don't forget your cover letter. Send it along with your résumé as a single message.

Scannable Résumés

Some companies are relying on technology to narrow the candidate pool for available job openings. Electronic Applicant Tracking uses imaging to scan, sort, and store résumé elements in a database. Then, through OCR (Optical Character Recognition) software, the computer scans the résumés for keywords and phrases. To have the best chance at getting an interview, you want to increase the number of "hits"—matches of your skills, abilities, experience, and education to those the computer is scanning for—your résumé will get. You can see how critical using the right keywords is for this type of résumé.

Technical considerations include:

- Again, do not use boldface (newer systems may be able to read this, but many older ones won't), italics, underlining, bullets, shading, graphics, or multiple font sizes. Instead, for emphasis, use asterisks, plus signs, or all capital letters. Minimize abbreviations.
- Use a popular typeface such as Courier, Helvetica, Ariel, or Palatino. Avoid decorative fonts.
- Font size should be between 11 and 14 points.
- Do not compress the spacing between letters.
- Use horizontal and vertical lines sparingly; the computer may misread them as the letters *L* or *I*.
- Left-justify the text.
- Do not use parentheses or brackets around telephone numbers, and be sure your phone number is on its own line of text.
- Your name should be the first line of text and on its own line. If your résumé is longer than one page, be sure to put your name on the top of all pages.
- Use a traditional résumé structure. The chronological format may work best.
- Use nouns that are skill-focused, such as *management, writer,* and *programming.* This is different from traditional paper résumés, which use action-oriented verbs.
- Laser printers produce the finest copies. Avoid dot-matrix printers.
- Use standard, light-colored paper with text on one side only. Since the higher the contrast, the better, your best choice is black ink on white paper.
- Always send original copies. If you must fax, set the fax on fine mode, not standard.
- Do not staple or fold your résumé. This can confuse the computer.
- Before you send your scannable résumé, be certain the employer uses this technology. If you can't determine this, you may want to send two versions (scannable and traditional) to be sure your résumé gets considered.

Résumé Production and Other Tips

An ink-jet printer is the preferred option for printing your résumé. Begin by printing just a few copies. You may find a small error or you may simply want to make some changes, and it is less frustrating and less expensive if you print in small batches.

Résumé paper color should be carefully chosen. You should consider the types of employers who will receive your résumé and the types of positions for which you are applying. Use white or ivory paper for traditional or conservative employers or for higher-level positions.

Black ink on sharp, white paper can be harsh on the reader's eyes. Think about an ivory or cream paper that will provide less contrast and be easier to read. Pink, green, and blue tints should generally be avoided.

Many résumé writers buy packages of matching envelopes and cover sheet stationery that, although not absolutely necessary, help convey a professional impression.

If you'll be producing many cover letters at home, be sure you have high-quality printing equipment. Learn standard envelope formats for business, and retain a copy of every cover letter you send out. You can use the copies to take notes of any telephone conversations that may occur.

If attending a job fair, either carry a briefcase or place your résumé in a nicely covered legal-size pad holder.

The Cover Letter

The cover letter provides you with the opportunity to tailor your résumé by telling the prospective employer how you can be a benefit to the organization. It allows you to highlight aspects of your background that are not already discussed in your résumé and that might be especially relevant to the organization you are contacting or to the position you are seeking. Every résumé should have a cover letter enclosed when you send it out. Unlike the résumé, which may be mass-produced, a cover letter is most effective when it is individually prepared and focused on the particular requirements of the organization in question.

A good cover letter should supplement the résumé and motivate the reader to review the résumé. The format shown in Exhibit 2.3 (see page 34) is only a suggestion to help you decide what information to include in a cover letter.

Begin the cover letter with your street address six lines down from the top. Leave three to five lines between the date and the name of the person to whom you are addressing the cover letter. Make sure you leave one blank line between the salutation and the body of the letter and between paragraphs. After typing "Sincerely," leave four blank lines and type your name. This should leave plenty of room for your signature. A sample cover letter is shown in Exhibit 2.4 on page 35.

The following guidelines will help you write good cover letters:

1. Be sure to type your letter neatly; ensure there are no misspellings.
2. Avoid unusual typefaces, such as script.
3. Address the letter to an individual, using the person's name and title. To obtain this information, call the company. If answering a blind newspaper advertisement, address the letter "To Whom It May Concern" or omit the salutation.
4. Be sure your cover letter directly indicates the position you are applying for and tells why you are qualified to fill it.
5. Send the original letter, not a photocopy, with your résumé. Keep a copy for your records.
6. Make your cover letter no more than one page.
7. Include a phone number where you can be reached.
8. Avoid trite language and have someone read the letter over to react to its tone, content, and mechanics.
9. For your own information, record the date you send out each letter and résumé.

Exhibit 2.3
COVER LETTER FORMAT

Your Street Address
Your Town, State, Zip
Phone Number
Fax Number
E-mail

Date

Name
Title
Organization
Address

Dear _____:

First Paragraph. In this paragraph state the reason for the letter, name the specific position or type of work you are applying for, and indicate from which resource (career services office, website, newspaper, contact, employment service) you learned of this opening. The first paragraph can also be used to inquire about future openings.

Second Paragraph. Indicate why you are interested in this position, the company, or its products or services and what you can do for the employer. If you are a recent graduate, explain how your academic background makes you a qualified candidate. Try not to repeat the same information found in the résumé.

Third Paragraph. Refer the reader to the enclosed résumé for more detailed information.

Fourth Paragraph. In this paragraph say what you will do to follow up on your letter. For example, state that you will call by a certain date to set up an interview or to find out if the company will be recruiting in your area. Finish by indicating your willingness to answer any questions the recipient may have. Be sure you have provided your phone number.

Sincerely,

Type your name

Enclosure

Exhibit 2.4
SAMPLE COVER LETTER

21 Bright Angel Terrace
Hilo, HA 96822
(808) 555-8478
kthernandez@site.com

February 12, 2007

Barbara Sapp-Yarwood
Human Resources Director
Scanlon Solutions
1507 Dannon Ave.
Cerritos, CA 90807

Dear Ms. Sapp-Yarwood:

Christine Yasso, a former coworker of mine and also your executive account manager, told me about your opening for a benefits specialist in the HR department. After working with Christine, I know Scanlon looks only for the best, and I believe I would be a good fit for the position and the company.

I have honed my skills at Kilauea Escape, a luxury resort near Hilo, splitting time between benefits work and corporate training/on-boarding, but before this year I handled benefits for Kilauea full-time and succeeded in creating win-win situations for employees and the company. By partnering with several larger resorts on the island, for example, I was able to secure less expensive health insurance through a Southern California firm while also improving overall coverage. I've also made it a point to offer our employees low-cost "lifestyle" benefits, such as allowing office personnel to bring dogs to work and rewarding outstanding performance with trade-out weekends at some of the same resorts we pooled with on our health plan.

I recognize that such unconventional perks wouldn't necessarily be appropriate in Scanlon's more corporate environment, but I feel I could bring the same innovative spirit and sense of goodwill to your HR team. Please see my résumé for more details on my record of cost management at Kilauea.

continued

I will be in LA at the end of February for a personal visit and would be interested in stopping by the office for a tour while I'm there, even if you've filled the position. Thanks for your consideration, and please let me know if I can answer any questions, whether by phone at (808) 555-8478 or by e-mail at kthernandez@site.com.

Sincerely,

Kaytlyn Hernandez

Enc.

3

Researching Careers and Networking

What do they call the job you want? One reason for confusion is perhaps a mistaken assumption that a college education provides job training. In most cases it does not. Of course, applied fields such as engineering, management, or education provide specific skills for the workplace as well as an education. Regardless, your overall college education exposes you to numerous fields of study and teaches you quantitative reasoning, critical thinking, writing, and speaking, all of which can be successfully applied to a number of different job fields. But it still remains up to you to choose a job field and to learn how to articulate the benefits of your education in a way the employer will appreciate.

What can you do with your degree? The choices really are limitless, which is one good reason to narrow the field while you're still in school. Your answers will determine where you should look, whether you'll need a postgraduate degree, and what sort of courses you should take in the meantime. Do you lean toward government? Finance? Banking? With the curriculum you've followed so far, any of these fields, and many others, might be appropriate. The decision rests with you, but the information you need to make it may be closer than you think. While your classes won't help you much with job research, there are probably a number of resources at the campus library that can help. Read on for some suggestions.

Collect Job Titles

The world of employment is a complex place, so you need to become a bit of an explorer and adventurer and be willing to try a variety of techniques to develop a list of possible occupations that might use your talents and education. You might find computerized interest inventories, reference books and other sources, and classified ads helpful in this respect. Once you have a list of possibilities that you are interested in and qualified for, you can move on to find out what kinds of organizations have these job titles.

Computerized Interest Inventories. One way to begin collecting job titles is to identify a number of jobs that call for your degree and the particular skills and interests you identified as part of the self-assessment process. There are excellent interactive career-guidance programs on the market to help you produce such selected lists of possible job titles. Most of these are available at colleges and at some larger town and city libraries. Two of the industry leaders are *CHOICES* and *DISCOVER*. Both allow you to enter interests, values, educational background, and other information to produce lists of possible occupations and industries. Each of the resources listed here will produce different job title lists. Some job titles will appear again and again, while others will be unique to a particular source. Investigate all of them!

Reference Sources. Books on the market that may be available through your local library or career counseling office also suggest various occupations related to specific majors. The following are only a few of the many good books on the market: *The College Board Guide to 150 Popular College Majors* and *College Majors and Careers: A Resource Guide for Effective Life Planning* both by Paul Phifer, and *Kaplan's What to Study: 101 Fields in a Flash*. All of these books list possible job titles within the academic major.

Not every employer seeking to hire an economist may be equally desirable to you. Work environments, even for the same type of employer and same position, vary from place to place. It pays to visit some of the types of offices you'd consider working in to get a feel for the culture and see whether you'd feel comfortable working there.

Observe not just the surroundings—everything from the conference rooms to the kinds of personal effects people keep at their desks—but the atmosphere. Is it noisy or quiet? Do coworkers drop by each other's offices to chat, or are they more formal? How are they dressed? Many workers cite atmosphere and the people they work with as big factors in how well they like their jobs. Internships and coops can help on both fronts. No career office or book can tell you what it will be like to work for a specific employer.

Each job title deserves your consideration. Like removing the layers of an onion, the search for job titles can go on and on! As you spend time doing this activity, you are actually learning more about the value of your degree. What's important in your search at this point is not to become critical or selective but rather to develop as long a list of possibilities as you can. Every source used will help you add new and potentially exciting jobs to your growing list.

Classified Ads. It has been well publicized that the classified ad section of the newspaper represents only a small fraction of the current job market. Nevertheless, the weekly classified ads can be a great help to you in your search. Although they may not be the best place to look for a job, they can teach you a lot about the job market. Classified ads provide a good education in job descriptions, duties, responsibilities, and qualifications. In addition, they provide insight into which industries are actively recruiting and some indication of the area's employment market. This is particularly helpful when seeking a position in a specific geographic area and/or a specific field. For your purposes, classified ads are a good source for job titles to add to your list.

Read the Sunday classified ads in a major market newspaper for several weeks in a row. Cut and paste all the ads that interest you and seem to call for something close to your education, skills, experience, and interests. Remember that classified ads are written for what an organization *hopes* to find; you don't have to meet absolutely every criterion. However, if certain requirements are stated as absolute minimums and you cannot meet them, it's best not to waste your time and that of the employer.

The weekly classified want ads exercise is important because these jobs are out in the marketplace. They truly exist, and people with your qualifications are being sought to apply. What's more, many of these advertisements describe the duties and responsibilities of the job advertised and give you a beginning sense of the challenges and opportunities such a position presents. Some will indicate salary, and that will be helpful as well. This information will better define the jobs for you and provide some good material for possible interviews in that field.

Explore Job Descriptions

Once you've arrived at a solid list of possible job titles that interest you and for which you believe you are somewhat qualified, it's a good idea to do some research on each of these jobs. The preeminent source for such job information is the *Dictionary of Occupational Titles*, or *DOT* (wave.net/upg/immigration/dot_index.html). This directory lists every conceivable job and provides excellent up-to-date information on duties and responsibilities, interactions with associates, and day-to-day assignments and tasks. These descriptions provide a thorough job analysis, but they do not consider the possible employers or the environments in which a job may be performed. So, although a position as public relations officer may be well defined in terms of duties and responsibilities, it does not explain the differences in doing public relations work in a college or a hospital or a factory or a bank. You will need to look somewhere else for work settings.

Learn More About Possible Work Settings

After reading some job descriptions, you may choose to edit and revise your list of job titles once again, discarding those you feel are not suitable and keeping those that continue to hold your interest. Or you may wish to keep your list intact and see where these jobs may be located. For example, if you are interested in public relations and you appear to have those skills and the requisite education, you'll want to know which organizations do public relations. How can you find that out? How much income does someone in public relations make a year and what is the employment potential for the field of public relations?

To answer these and many other questions about your list of job titles, we recommend you try any of the following resources: *Careers Encyclopedia*, the professional societies and resources found throughout this book, *College to Career: The Guide to Job Opportunities*, and the *Occupational Outlook Handbook* (http://stats.bls.gov/ocohome.htm). Each of these resources, in a different way, will help to put the job titles you have selected into an employer context. Perhaps the most extensive discussion is found in the *Occupational Outlook Handbook*, which gives a thorough presentation of the nature of the work, the working conditions, employment statistics, training, other qualifications, and advancement possibilities as well as job outlook and earnings. Related occupations are also detailed, and a select bibliography is provided to help you find additional information.

Continuing with our public relations example, your search through these reference materials would teach you that the public relations jobs you find attractive are available in larger hospitals, financial institutions, most corporations (both consumer goods and industrial goods), media organizations, and colleges and universities.

Networking

Networking is the process of deliberately establishing relationships to get career-related information or to alert potential employers that you are available for work. Networking is critically important to today's job seeker for two reasons: It will help you get the information you need, and it can help you find out about *all* of the available jobs.

Get the Information You Need

Networkers will review your résumé and give you feedback on its effectiveness. They will talk about the job you are looking for and give you a candid appraisal of how they see your strengths and weaknesses. If they have a good sense of the industry or the employment sector for that job, you'll get their feelings on future trends in the industry as well. Some networkers will be very forthcoming about salaries, job-hunting techniques, and suggestions for your job search strategy. Many have been known to place calls right from the interview desk to friends and associates who might be interested in you. Each networker will make his or her own contribution, and each will be valuable.

Because organizations must evolve to adapt to current global market needs, the information provided by decision makers within various organizations will be critical to your success as a new job market entrant. For example, you might learn about the concept of virtual organizations from a networker. Virtual organizations coordinate economic activity to deliver value to customers by using resources outside the traditional boundaries of the organization. This concept is being discussed and implemented by chief executive officers of many organizations, including Ford Motor, Dell, and IBM. Networking can help you find out about this and other trends currently affecting the industries under your consideration.

Find Out About All of the Available Jobs

Not every job that is available at this very moment is advertised for potential applicants to see. This is called the *hidden job market*. Only 15 to 20 percent of all jobs are formally advertised, which means that 80 to 85 percent of available jobs do not appear in published channels. Networking will help you become more knowledgeable about all the employment opportunities available during your job search period.

Although someone you might talk to today doesn't know of any openings within his or her organization, tomorrow or next week or next month an opening may occur. If you've taken the time to show an interest in and knowledge of their organization, if you've shown the company representative how you can help achieve organizational goals and that you can fit into the organization, you'll be one of the first candidates considered for the position.

Networking: A Proactive Approach

Networking is a proactive rather than a reactive approach. You, as a job seeker, are expected to initiate a certain level of activity on your own behalf; you cannot afford to simply respond to jobs listed in the newspaper. Being proactive means building a network of contacts that includes informed and interested decision makers who will provide you with up-to-date knowledge of the current job market and increase your chances of finding out about employment opportunities appropriate for your interests, experience, and level of education. An old axiom of networking says, "You are only two phone calls away from the information you need." In other words, by talking to enough people, you will quickly come across someone who can offer you help.

Preparing to Network

In deliberately establishing relationships, maximize your efforts by organizing your approach. Five specific areas in which you can organize your efforts include reviewing your self-assessment, reviewing your research on job sites and organizations, deciding who you want to talk to, keeping track of all your efforts, and creating your self-promotion tools.

Review Your Self-Assessment

Your self-assessment is as important a tool in preparing to network as it has been in other aspects of your job search. You have carefully evaluated your personal traits, personal values, economic needs, longer-term goals, skill base, preferred skills, and underdeveloped skills. During the networking process you will be called upon to communicate what you know about yourself and relate it to the information or job you seek. Be sure to review the exercises that you completed in the self-assessment section of this book in preparation for networking. We've explained that you need to assess which skills you have acquired from your major that are of general value to an employer;

be ready to express those in ways he or she can appreciate as useful in the organizations.

Review Research on Job Sites and Organizations

In addition, individuals assisting you will expect that you'll have at least some background information on the occupation or industry of interest to you. Refer to the appropriate sections of this book and other relevant publications to acquire the background information necessary for effective networking. They'll explain how to identify not only the job titles that might be of interest to you but also which kinds of organizations employ people to do that job. You will develop some sense of working conditions and expectations about duties and responsibilities—all of which will be of help in your networking interviews.

Decide Who You Want to Talk To

Networking cannot begin until you decide who you want to talk to and, in general, what type of information you hope to gain from your contacts. Once you know this, it's time to begin developing a list of contacts. Five useful sources for locating contacts are described here.

College Alumni Network. Most colleges and universities have created a formal network of alumni and friends of the institution who are particularly interested in helping currently enrolled students and graduates of their alma mater gain employment-related information.

It is usually a simple process to make use of an alumni network. Visit your college's website and locate the alumni office and/or your career center. Either or both sites will have information about your school's alumni network. You'll be provided with information on shadowing experiences, geographic information, or those alumni offering job referrals. If you don't find what you're looking for, don't hesitate to phone or e-mail your career center and ask what they can do to help you connect with an alum.

Alumni networkers may provide some combination of the following services: day-long shadowing experiences, telephone interviews, in-person interviews, information on relocating to given geographic areas, internship information, suggestions on graduate school study, and job vacancy notices.

Present and Former Supervisors. If you believe you are on good terms with present or former job supervisors, they may be an excellent resource for providing information or directing you to appropriate resources that would have information related to your current interests and needs. Additionally, these supervisors probably belong to professional organizations that they might be willing to utilize to get information for you.

Employers in Your Area. Although you may be interested in working in a geographic location different from the one where you currently reside, don't overlook the value of the knowledge and contacts those around you are able to provide. Use the local telephone directory and newspaper to identify the types of organizations you are thinking of working for or professionals who have the kinds of jobs you are interested in. Recently, a call made to a local hospital's financial administrator for information on working in health-care financial administration yielded more pertinent information on training seminars, regional professional organizations, and potential employment sites than a national organization was willing to provide.

Employers in Geographic Areas Where You Hope to Work. If you are thinking about relocating, identifying prospective employers or informational contacts in the new location will be critical to your success. Here are some tips for online searching. First, use a "metasearch" engine to get the most out of your search. Metasearch engines combine several engines into one powerful tool. We frequently use dogpile.com and metasearch.com for this purpose. Try using the city and state as your keywords in a search. *New Haven, Connecticut* will bring you to the city's website with links to the chamber of commerce, member businesses, and other valuable resources. By using looksmart.com you can locate newspapers in any area, and they, too, can provide valuable insight before you relocate. Of course, both dogpile and metasearch can lead you to yellow and white page directories in areas you are considering.

Professional Associations and Organizations. Professional associations and organizations can provide valuable information in several areas: career paths that you might not have considered, qualifications relating to those career choices, publications that list current job openings, and workshops or seminars that will enhance your professional knowledge and skills. They can also be excellent sources for background information on given industries: their health, current problems, and future challenges.

There are several excellent resources available to help you locate professional associations and organizations that would have information to meet your needs. Two especially useful publications are the *Encyclopedia of Associations* and *National Trade and Professional Associations of the United States*.

Keep Track of All Your Efforts

It can be difficult, almost impossible, to remember all the details related to each contact you make during the networking process, so you will want to develop a record-keeping system that works for you. Formalize this process by using your computer to keep a record of the people and organizations you want to contact. You can simply record the contact's name, address, and telephone number, and what information you hope to gain.

You could record this as a simple Word document and you could still use the "Find" function if you were trying to locate some data and could only recall the firm's name or the contact's name. If you're comfortable with database management and you have some database software on your computer, then you can put information at your fingertips even if you have only the zip code! The point here is not technological sophistication but good record keeping.

Once you have created this initial list, it will be helpful to keep more detailed information as you begin to actually make the contacts. Those details should include complete contact information, the date and content of each contact, names and information for additional networkers, and required follow-up. Don't forget to send a letter thanking your contact for his or her time! Your contact will appreciate your recall of details of your meetings and conversations, and the information will help you to focus your networking efforts.

Create Your Self-Promotion Tools

There are two types of promotional tools that are used in the networking process. The first is a résumé and cover letter, and the second is a one-minute "infomercial," which may be given over the telephone or in person.

Techniques for writing an effective résumé and cover letter are discussed in Chapter 2. Once you have reviewed that material and prepared these important documents, you will have created one of your self-promotion tools.

The one-minute infomercial will demand that you begin tying your interests, abilities, and skills to the people or organizations you want to network with. Think about your goal for making the contact to help you understand what you should say about yourself. You should be able to express yourself easily and convincingly. If, for example, you are contacting an alumnus of your institution to obtain the names of possible employment sites in a distant city, be prepared to discuss why you are interested in moving to that location, the types of jobs you are interested in, and the skills and abilities you possess that will make you a qualified candidate.

To create a meaningful one-minute infomercial, write it out, practice it as if it will be a spoken presentation, rewrite it, and practice it again if necessary until expressing yourself comes easily and is convincing.

Here's a simplified example of an infomercial for use over the telephone:

Ms. Berger, my name is Prakash Patel, and I'm calling to find out whether you would have time to sit down with me for thirty minutes and give me your take on economics careers. I just graduated from Washington University, and I'm looking for job openings as an economic analyst. I know you've spent a lot of time working at the state level in that position, and I'm hoping to learn from your experience and find out what it's really like out in the field. There are so many options, and talking with you sould give me a better handle on which path I should follow.

I interned with the Department of Labor last summer and also minored in statistics, so I think I have the background necessary to do the work. But I'd be interested in hearing more about your education, advancement, and where you see the field headed and what steps would best prepare me for that.

Would you have any time next week? I'm available during the day or after-hours and could stop by your office. Thanks so much for the help.

It very well may happen that your employer contact wishes you to communicate by e-mail. The infomercial quoted above could easily be rewritten for an e-mail message. You should "cut and paste" your résumé right into the e-mail text itself.

Other effective self-promotion tools include portfolios for those in the arts, writing professions, or teaching. Portfolios show examples of work, photographs of projects or classroom activities, or certificates and credentials that are job related. There may not be an opportunity to use the portfolio during an interview, and it is not something that should be left with the organization. It is designed to be explained and displayed by the creator. However, during some networking meetings, there may be an opportunity to illustrate a point or strengthen a qualification by exhibiting the portfolio.

Beginning the Networking Process

Set the Tone for Your Communications

It can be useful to establish "tone words" for any communications you embark upon. Before making your first telephone call or writing your first letter, decide what you want the person to think of you. If you are networking to try to obtain a job, your tone words might include descriptors such as *genuine*, *informed*, and *self-knowledgeable*. When you're trying to acquire information, your tone words may have a slightly different focus, such as *courteous*, *organized*, *focused*, and *well-spoken*. Use the tone words you establish for your contacts to guide you through the networking process.

Honestly Express Your Intentions

When contacting individuals, it is important to be honest about your reasons for making the contact. Establish your purpose in your own mind and be able and ready to articulate it concisely. Determine an initial agenda, whether it be informational questioning or self-promotion, present it to your contact, and be ready to respond immediately. If you don't adequately prepare before initiating your overture, you may find yourself at a disadvantage if you're asked to immediately begin your informational interview or self-promotion during the first phone conversation or visit.

Start Networking within Your Circle of Confidence

Once you have organized your approach—by utilizing specific researching methods, creating a system for keeping track of the people you will contact, and developing effective self-promotion tools—you are ready to begin networking. The best way to begin networking is by talking with a group of people you trust and feel comfortable with. This group is usually made up of your family, friends, and career counselors. No matter who is in this inner circle, they will have a special interest in seeing you succeed in your job search. In addition, because they will be easy to talk to, you should try taking some risks in terms of practicing your information-seeking approach. Gain confidence in talking about the strengths you bring to an organization and the underdeveloped skills you feel hinder your candidacy. Be sure to review the section on self-assessment for tips on approaching each of these areas. Ask for critical but constructive feedback from the people in your circle of confidence on the letters you write and the one-minute infomercial you have developed. Evaluate whether you want to make the changes they suggest, then practice the changes on others within this circle.

Stretch the Boundaries of Your Networking Circle of Confidence

Once you have refined the promotional tools you will use to accomplish your networking goals, you will want to make additional contacts. Because you will not know most of these people, it will be a less comfortable activity to undertake. The practice that you gained with your inner circle of trusted friends should have prepared you to now move outside of that comfort zone.

It is said that any information a person needs is only two phone calls away, but the information cannot be gained until you (1) make a reasonable guess about who might have the information you need and (2) pick up the telephone to make the call. Using your network list that includes alumni, instructors, supervisors, employers, and associations, you can begin preparing your list of questions that will allow you to get the information you need.

Prepare the Questions You Want to Ask

Networkers can provide you with the insider's perspective on any given field and you can ask them questions that you might not want to ask in an interview. For example, you can ask them to describe the more repetitious or mundane parts of the job or ask them for a realistic idea of salary expectations. Be sure to prepare your questions ahead of time so that you are organized and efficient.

Be Prepared to Answer Some Questions

To communicate effectively, you must anticipate questions that will be asked of you by the networkers you contact. Revisit the self-assessment process you undertook and the research you've done so that you can effortlessly respond to questions about your short- and long-term goals and the kinds of jobs you are most interested in pursuing.

General Networking Tips

Make Every Contact Count. Setting the tone for each interaction is critical. Approaches that will help you communicate in an effective way include politeness, being appreciative of time provided to you, and being prepared and thorough. Remember, *everyone* within an organization has a circle of influence, so be prepared to interact effectively with each person you encounter in the networking process, including secretarial and support staff. Many information or job seekers have thwarted their own efforts by being rude to some individuals they encountered as they networked because they made the incorrect assumption that certain persons were unimportant.

Sometimes your contacts may be surprised at their ability to help you. After meeting and talking with you, they might think they have not offered much in the way of help. A day or two later, however, they may make a contact that would be useful to you and refer you to that person.

With Each Contact, Widen Your Circle of Networkers. Always leave an informational interview with the names of at least two more people who can help you get the information or job that you are seeking. Don't be shy about asking for additional contacts; networking is all about increasing the number of people you can interact with to achieve your goals.

Make Your Own Decisions. As you talk with different people and get answers to the questions you pose, you may hear conflicting information or get conflicting suggestions. Your job is to listen to these "experts" and decide what information and which suggestions will help you achieve *your* goals. Only implement those suggestions that you believe will work for you.

Shutting Down Your Network

As you achieve the goals that motivated your networking activity—getting the information you need or the job you want—the time will come to inactivate all or parts of your network. As you do, be sure to tell your primary supporters about your change in status. Call or write to each one of them and give them as many details about your new status as you feel is necessary to maintain a positive relationship.

Because a network takes on a life of its own, activity undertaken on your behalf will continue even after you cease your efforts. As you get calls or are contacted in some fashion, be sure to inform these networkers about your change in status, and thank them for assistance they have provided.

Information on the latest employment trends indicates that workers will change jobs or careers several times in their lifetime. Networking, then, will be a critical aspect in the span of your professional life. If you carefully and thoughtfully conduct your networking activities during your job search, you will have a solid foundation of experience when you need to network the next time around.

Where Are These Jobs, Anyway?

Having a list of job titles that you've designed around your own career interests and skills is an excellent beginning. It means you've really thought about who you are and what you are presenting to the employment market. It has caused you to think seriously about the most appealing environments to work in, and you have identified some employer types that represent these environments.

The research and the thinking that you've done thus far will be used again and again. They will be helpful in writing your résumé and cover letters, in talking about yourself on the telephone to prospective employers, and in answering interview questions.

Now is a good time to begin to narrow the field of job titles and employment sites down to some specific employers to initiate the employment contact.

Find Out Which Employers Hire People Like You

This section will provide tips, techniques, and specific resources for developing an actual list of specific employers that can be used to make contacts. It is only an outline that you must be prepared to tailor to your own particular needs and according to what you bring to the job search. Once again, it is important to communicate with others along the way exactly what you're looking for and what your goals are for the research you're doing. Librarians, employers, career counselors, friends, friends of friends, business contacts, and bookstore staff will all have helpful information on geographically specific and new resources to aid you in locating employers who'll hire you.

Identify Information Resources

Your interview wardrobe and your new résumé might have put a dent in your wallet, but the resources you'll need to pursue your job search are available for free. The categories of information detailed here are not hard to find and are yours for the browsing.

Numerous resources described in this section will help you identify actual employers. Use all of them or any others that you identify as available in your geographic area. As you become experienced in this process, you'll quickly figure out which information sources are helpful and which are not. If you live in a rural area, a well-planned day trip to a major city that includes a college career office, a large college or city library, state and federal employment centers, a chamber of commerce office, and a well-stocked bookstore can produce valuable results.

There are many excellent resources available to help you identify actual job sites. They are categorized into employer directories (usually indexed by product lines and geographic location), geographically based directories (designed to highlight particular cities, regions, or states), career-specific directories (e.g., *Sports MarketPlace*, which lists tens of thousands of firms involved with sports), periodicals and newspapers, targeted job posting publications, and videos. This is by no means meant to be a complete treatment of resources but rather a starting point for identifying useful resources.

Working from the more general references to highly specific resources, we provide a basic list to help you begin your search. Many of these you'll find easily available. In some cases reference librarians and others will suggest even better materials for your particular situation. Start to create your own customized bibliography of job search references.

Geographically Based Directories. The Job Bank series published by Bob Adams, Inc. (aip.com) contains detailed entries on each area's major employers, including business activity, address, phone number, and hiring contact name. Many listings specify educational backgrounds being sought in potential employees. Each volume contains a solid discussion of each city's or state's major employment sectors. Organizations are also indexed by industry. Job Bank volumes are available for the following places: Atlanta, Boston, Chicago, Dallas–Ft. Worth, Denver, Detroit, Florida, Houston, Los Angeles, Minneapolis, New York, Ohio, Philadelphia, San Francisco, Seattle, St. Louis, Washington, D.C., and other cities throughout the Northwest.

National Job Bank (careercity.com) lists employers in every state, along with contact names and commonly hired job categories. Included are many small companies often overlooked by other directories. Companies are also indexed by industry. This publication provides information on educational backgrounds sought and lists company benefits.

Periodicals and Newspapers. Several sources are available to help you locate which journals or magazines carry job advertisements in your field. Other resources help you identify opportunities in other parts of the country.

- *Where the Jobs Are: A Comprehensive Directory of 1,200 Journals Listing Career Opportunities*
- *Corptech Fast 5,000 Company Locator*
- *National Ad Search* (nationaladsearch.com)
- *The Federal Jobs Digest* (jobsfed.com) and *Federal Career Opportunities*
- *World Chamber of Commerce Directory* (chamberofcommerce.org)

This list is certainly not exhaustive; use it to begin your job search work.

Targeted Job Posting Publications. Although the resources that follow are national in scope, they are either targeted to one medium of contact (telephone), focused on specific types of jobs, or less comprehensive than the sources previously listed.

- Careers.org (careers.org/index.html)
- *The Job Hunter* (jobhunter.com)
- *Current Jobs for Graduates* (graduatejobs.com)
- *Environmental Opportunities* (ecojobs.com)
- *Y National Vacancy List* (ymca.net/employment/ymca_recruiting/ jobright.htm)
- *ArtSEARCH*
- *Community Jobs*
- *National Association of Colleges and Employers: Job Choices series*
- *National Association of Colleges and Employers* (jobweb.com)

Videos. You may be one of the many job seekers who likes to get information via a medium other than paper. Many career libraries, public libraries, and career centers in libraries carry an assortment of videos that will help you learn new techniques and get information helpful in the job search.

Locate Information Resources

Throughout these introductory chapters, we have continually referred you to various websites for information on everything from job listings to career information. Using the Web gives you a mobility at your computer that you don't enjoy if you rely solely on books or newspapers or printed journals. Moreover, material on the Web, if the site is maintained, can be the most up-to-date information available.

You'll eventually identify the information resources that work best for you, but make certain you've covered the full range of resources before you begin to rely on a smaller list. Here's a short list of informational sites that many job seekers find helpful:

- Public and college libraries
- College career centers
- Bookstores
- The Internet
- Local and state government personnel offices
- Career/job fairs

Each one of these sites offers a collection of resources that will help you get the information you need.

As you meet and talk with service professionals at all these sites, be sure to let them know what you're doing. Inform them of your job search, what you've already accomplished, and what you're looking for. The more people who know you're job seeking, the greater the possibility that someone will have information or know someone who can help you along your way.

Interviewing and
Job Offer Considerations

Certainly, there can be no one part of the job search process more fraught with anxiety and worry than the interview. Yet seasoned job seekers welcome the interview and will often say, "Just get me an interview and I'm on my way!" They understand that the interview is crucial to the hiring process and equally crucial for them, as job candidates, to have the opportunity of a personal dialogue to add to what the employer may already have learned from the résumé, cover letter, and telephone conversations.

Believe it or not, the interview is to be welcomed, and even enjoyed! It is a perfect opportunity for you, the candidate, to sit down with an employer and express yourself and display who you are and what you want. Of course, it takes thought and planning and a little strategy; after all, it *is* a job interview! But it can be a positive, if not pleasant, experience and one you can look back on and feel confident about your performance and effort.

For many new job seekers, a job, any job, seems a wonderful thing. But seasoned interview veterans know that the job interview is an important step for both sides—the employer and the candidate—to see what each has to offer and whether there is going to be a "fit" of personalities, work styles, and attitudes. And it is this concept of balance in the interview, that both sides have important parts to play, that holds the key to success in mastering this aspect of the job search strategy.

Try to think of the interview as a conversation between two interested and equal partners. You both have important, even vital, information to deliver and to learn. Of course, there's no denying the employer has some leverage, especially in the initial interview for recruitment or any interview scheduled by the candidate and not the recruiter. That should not prevent the interviewee from seeking to play an equal part in what should be a fair exchange of information. Too often the untutored candidate allows the interview to become one-sided. The employer asks all the questions and the candidate simply responds. The ideal would be for two mutually interested parties to sit down and discuss possibilities for each. This is a conversation of significance, and it requires preparation, thought about the tone of the interview, and planning of the nature and details of the information to be exchanged.

Preparing for the Interview

The length of most initial interviews is about thirty minutes. Given the brevity, the information that is exchanged ought to be important. The candidate should be delivering material that the employer cannot discover on the résumé, and in turn, the candidate should be learning things about the employer that he or she could not otherwise find out. After all, if you have only thirty minutes, why waste time on information that is already published? The information exchanged is more than just factual, and both sides will learn much from what they see of each other, as well. How the candidate looks, speaks, and acts are important to the employer. The employer's attention to the interview and awareness of the candidate's résumé, the setting, and the quality of information presented are important to the candidate.

Just as the employer has every right to be disappointed when a prospect is late for the interview, looks unkempt, and seems ill-prepared to answer fairly standard questions, the candidate may be disappointed with an interviewer who isn't ready for the meeting, hasn't learned the basic résumé facts, and is constantly interrupted by telephone calls. In either situation there's good reason to feel let down.

There are many elements to a successful interview, and some of them are not easy to describe or prepare for. Sometimes there is just a chemistry between interviewer and interviewee that brings out the best in both, and a good exchange takes place. But there is much the candidate can do to pave the way for success in terms of his or her résumé, personal appearance, goals, and interview strategy—each of which we will discuss. However, none of this preparation is as important as the time and thought the candidate gives to personal self-assessment.

Self-Assessment

Neither a stunning résumé nor an expensive, well-tailored suit can compensate for candidates who do not know what they want, where they are going, or why they are interviewing with a particular employer. Self-assessment, the process by which we begin to know and acknowledge our own particular blend of education, experiences, needs, and goals, is not something that can be sorted out the weekend before a major interview. Of all the elements of interview preparation, this one requires the longest lead time and cannot be faked.

Because the time allotted for most interviews is brief, it is all the more important for job candidates to understand and express succinctly why they are there and what they have to offer. This is not a time for undue modesty (or for braggadocio either); it is a time for a compelling, reasoned statement of why you feel that you and this employer might make a good match. It means you have to have thought about your skills, interests, and attributes; related those to your life experiences and your own history of challenges and opportunities; and determined what that indicates about your strengths, preferences, values, and areas needing further development.

If you need some assistance with self-assessment issues, refer to Chapter 1. Included are suggested exercises that can be done as needed, such as making up an experiential diary and extracting obvious strengths and weaknesses from past experiences. These simple assignments will help you look at past activities as collections of tasks with accompanying skills and responsibilities. Don't overlook your high school or college career office. Many offer personal counseling on self-assessment issues and may provide testing instruments such as the *Myers-Briggs Type Indicator (MBTI)*, the *Harrington-O'Shea Career Decision-Making System (CDM)*, the *Strong Interest Inventory (SII)*, or any other of a wide selection of assessment tools that can help you clarify some of these issues prior to the interview stage of your job search.

The Résumé

Résumé preparation has been discussed in detail, and some basic examples were provided. In this section we want to concentrate on how best to use your résumé in the interview. In most cases the employer will have seen the résumé prior to the interview, and, in fact, it may well have been the quality of that résumé that secured the interview opportunity.

An interview is a conversation, however, and not an exercise in reading. So, if the employer hasn't seen your résumé and you have brought it along to the interview, wait until asked or until the end of the interview to offer it. Otherwise, you may find yourself staring at the back of your résumé and simply answering "yes" and "no" to a series of questions drawn from that document.

Sometimes an interviewer is not prepared and does not know or recall the contents of the résumé and may use the résumé to a greater or lesser degree as a "prompt" during the interview. It is for you to judge what that may indicate about the individual performing the interview or the employer. If your interviewer seems surprised by the scheduled meeting, relies on the résumé to an inordinate degree, and seems otherwise unfamiliar with your background, this lack of preparation for the hiring process could well be a symptom of general management disorganization or may simply be the result of poor planning on the part of one individual. It is your responsibility as a potential employee to be aware of these signals and make your decisions accordingly.

If you find that the interviewer is reading from your résumé rather than discussing the job with you, you can guide the interviewer back to the job dialogue by saying, "Mr. Davis, I would like to elaborate on the experience I gained in an internship that is not detailed on my résumé." This strategy may give you an opportunity to convey more information about your strengths and weaknesses and will reengage the direction of your interview.

By all means, bring at least one copy of your résumé to the interview. Occasionally, at the close of an interview, an interviewer will express an interest in circulating a résumé to several departments, and you could then offer the copy you brought. Sometimes, an interview appointment provides an opportunity to meet others in the organization who may express an interest in you and your background, and it may be helpful to follow up with a copy of your résumé. Our best advice, however, is to keep it out of sight until needed or requested.

Employer Information

Whether your interview is for graduate school admission, an overseas corporate position, or a position with a local company, it is important to know something about the employer or the organization. Keeping in mind that the interview is relatively brief and that you will hopefully have other interviews with other organizations, it is important to keep your research in proportion. If secondary interviews are called for, you will have additional time to do further research. For the first interview, it is helpful to know the organization's mission, goals, size, scope of operations, and so forth. Your research may uncover recent areas of challenge or particular successes that may help to fuel the interview. Use the "What Do They Call the Job

You Want?" section of Chapter 3, your library, and your career or guidance office to help you locate this information in the most efficient way possible. Don't be shy in asking advice of these counseling and guidance professionals on how best to spend your preparation time. With some practice, you'll soon learn how much information is enough and which kinds of information are most useful to you.

Interview Content

We've already discussed how it can help to think of the interview as an important conversation—one that, as with any conversation, you want to find pleasant and interesting and to leave you with a good feeling. But because this conversation is especially important, the information that's exchanged is critical to its success. What do you want them to know about you? What do you need to know about them? What interview technique do you need to particularly pay attention to? How do you want to manage the close of the interview? What steps will follow in the hiring process?

Except for the professional interviewer, most of us find interviewing stressful and anxiety-provoking. Developing a strategy before you begin interviewing will help you relieve some stress and anxiety. One particular strategy that has worked for many and may work for you is interviewing by objective. Before you interview, write down three to five goals you would like to achieve for that interview. They may be technique goals: smile a little more, have a firmer handshake, be sure to ask about the next stage in the interview process before leaving. They may be content-oriented goals: Find out about the company's current challenges and opportunities; be sure to speak of your recent research, writing experiences, or foreign travel. Whatever your goals, jot down a few of them as goals for each interview.

Most people find that in trying to achieve these few goals, their interviewing technique becomes more organized and focused. After the interview, the most common question friends and family ask is "How did it go?" With this technique, you have an indication of whether you met *your* goals for the meeting, not just some vague idea of how it went. Chances are, if you accomplished what you wanted to, it improved the quality of the entire interview. As you continue to interview, you will want to revise your goals to continue improving your interview skills.

Now, add to the concept of the significant conversation the idea of a beginning, a middle, and a closing and you will have two thoughts that will give your interview a distinctive character. Be sure to make your introduction warm and cordial. Say your full name (and if it's a difficult-to-pronounce name, help the interviewer to pronounce it) and make certain you know your interviewer's name and how to pronounce it. Most interviews begin with some "soft talk" about the weather, chat about the candidate's trip to the interview site, or national events. This is done as a courtesy to relax both you and the interviewer, to get you talking, and to generally try to defuse the atmosphere of excessive tension. Try to be yourself, engage in the conversation, and don't try to second-guess the interviewer. This is simply what it appears to be—casual conversation.

Once you and the interviewer move on to exchange more serious information in the middle part of the interview, the two most important concerns become your ability to handle challenging questions and your success at asking meaningful ones. Interviewer questions will probably fall into one of three categories: personal assessment and career direction, academic assessment, and knowledge of the employer. Here are a few examples of questions in each category:

Personal Assessment and Career Direction
1. What motivates you to put forth your best effort?
2. What do you consider to be your greatest strengths and weaknesses?
3. What qualifications do you have that make you think you will be successful in this career?

Academic Assessment
1. What led you to choose your major?
2. What subjects did you like best and least? Why?
3. How has your college experience prepared you for this career?

Knowledge of the Employer
1. What do you think it takes to be successful in an organization like ours?
2. In what ways do you think you can make a contribution to our organization?
3. Why did you choose to seek a position with this organization?

The interviewer wants a response to each question but is also gauging your enthusiasm, preparedness, and willingness to communicate. In each response you should provide some information about yourself that can be related to the employer's needs. A common mistake is to give too much information. Answer each question completely, but be careful not to run on too long with extensive details or examples.

Questions About Underdeveloped Skills

Most employers interview people who have met some minimum criteria of education and experience. They interview candidates to see who they are, to learn what kind of personality they exhibit, and to get some sense of how they might fit into the existing organization. It may be that you are asked about skills the employer hopes to find and that you have not documented. Maybe it's grant-writing experience, knowledge of the European political system, or a knowledge of the film world.

To questions about skills and experiences you don't have, answer honestly and forthrightly and try to offer some additional information about skills you do have. For example, perhaps the employer is disappointed you have no grant-writing experience. An honest answer may be as follows:

No, unfortunately, I was never in a position to acquire those skills. I do understand something of the complexities of the grant-writing process and feel confident that my attention to detail, careful reading skills, and strong writing would make grants a wonderful challenge in a new job. I think I could get up on the learning curve quickly.

The employer hears an honest admission of lack of experience but is reassured by some specific skill details that do relate to grant writing and a confident manner that suggests enthusiasm and interest in a challenge.

For many students, questions about their possible contribution to an employer's organization can prove challenging. Because your education has probably not included specific training for a job, you need to review your academic record and select capabilities you have developed in your major that an employer can appreciate. For example, perhaps you read well and can analyze and condense what you've read into smaller, more focused pieces. That could be valuable. Or maybe you did some serious research and you know you have valuable investigative skills. Your public speaking might be highly developed and you might use visual aids appropriately and effectively. Or maybe your skill at correspondence, memos, and messages is effective. Whatever it is, you must take it out of the academic context and put it into a new, employer-friendly context so your interviewer can best judge how you could help the organization.

Exhibiting knowledge of the organization will, without a doubt, show the interviewer that you are interested enough in the available position to have done some legwork in preparation for the interview. Remember, it is not necessary to know every detail of the organization's history but rather to have a general knowledge about why it is in business and how the industry is faring.

Sometime during the interview, generally after the midway point, you'll be asked if you have any questions for the interviewer. Your questions will tell the employer much about your attitude and your desire to understand the organization's expectations so you can compare them to your own strengths. The following are just a few questions you might want to ask:

1. What is the communication style of the organization? (meetings, memos, and so forth)
2. What would a typical day in this position be like for me?
3. What have been some of the interesting challenges and opportunities your organization has recently faced?

Most interviews draw to a natural closing point, so be careful not to prolong the discussion. At a signal from the interviewer, wind up your presentation, express your appreciation for the opportunity, and be sure to ask what the next stage in the process will be. When can you expect to hear from them? Will they be conducting second-tier interviews? If you are interested and haven't heard, would they mind a phone call? Be sure to collect a business card with the name and phone number of your interviewer. On your way out, you might have an opportunity to pick up organizational literature you haven't seen before.

With the right preparation—a thorough self-assessment, professional clothing, and employer information—you'll be able to set and achieve the goals you have established for the interview process.

Interview Follow-Up

Quite often there is a considerable time lag between interviewing for a position and being hired or, in the case of the networker, between your phone call or letter to a possible contact and the opportunity of a meeting. This can be frustrating. "Why aren't they contacting me?" "I thought I'd get another interview, but no one has telephoned." "Am I out of the running?" You don't know what is happening.

Consider the Differing Perspectives

Of course, there is another perspective—that of the networker or hiring organization. Organizations are complex, with multiple tasks that need to be accomplished each day. Hiring is a discrete activity that does not occur as frequently as other job assignments. The hiring process might have to take second place to other, more immediate organizational needs. Although it may be very important to you, and it is certainly ultimately significant to the employer, other issues such as fiscal management, planning and product development, employer vacation periods, or financial constraints may prevent an organization or individual within that organization from acting on your employment or your request for information as quickly as you or they would prefer.

Use Your Communications Skills

Good communication is essential here to resolve any anxieties, and the responsibility is on you, the job or information seeker. Too many job seekers and networkers offer as an excuse that they don't want to "bother" the organization by writing letters or calling. Let us assure you here and now, once and for all, that if you are troubling an organization by overcommunicating, someone will indicate that situation to you quite clearly. If not, you can only assume you are a worthwhile prospect and the employer appreciates being reminded of your availability and interest. Let's look at follow-up practices in the job interview process and the networking situation separately.

Following Up on the Employment Interview

A brief thank-you note following an interview is an excellent and polite way to begin a series of follow-up communications with a potential employer with whom you have interviewed and want to remain in touch. It should be just that—a thank-you for a good meeting. If you failed to mention some fact or experience during your interview that you think might add to your candidacy, you may use this note to do that. However, this should be essentially a note whose overall tone is appreciative and, if appropriate, indicative of a continuing interest in pursuing any opportunity that may exist with that organization. It is one of the few pieces of business correspondence that may be handwritten, but always use plain, good-quality, standard-size paper.

If, however, at this point you are no longer interested in the employer, the thank-you note is an appropriate time to indicate that. You are under no obligation to identify any reason for not continuing to pursue employment with that organization, but if you are so inclined to indicate your professional reasons (pursuing other employers more akin to your interests, looking for greater income production than this employer can provide, a different geographic location), you certainly may. It should not be written with an eye to negotiation, for it will not be interpreted as such.

As part of your interview closing, you should have taken the initiative to establish lines of communication for continuing information about your candidacy. If you asked permission to telephone, wait a week following your thank-you note, then telephone your contact simply to inquire how things are progressing on your employment status. The feedback you receive here should be taken at face value. If your interviewer simply has no information, he or she will tell you so and indicate whether you should call again and when. Don't be discouraged if this should continue over some period of time.

If during this time something occurs that you think improves or changes your candidacy (some new qualification or experience you may have had), including any offers from other organizations, by all means telephone or write to inform the employer about this. In the case of an offer from a competing but less desirable or equally desirable organization, telephone your contact, explain what has happened, express your real interest in the organization, and inquire whether some determination on your employment might be made before you must respond to this other offer. An organization that is truly interested in you may be moved to make a decision about your candidacy. Equally possible is the scenario in which they are not yet ready to make a decision and so advise you to take the offer that has been presented. Again, you have no ethical alternative but to deal with the information presented in a straightforward manner.

When accepting other employment, be sure to contact any employers still actively considering you and inform them of your new job. Thank them graciously for their consideration. There are many other job seekers out there just like you who will benefit from having their candidacy improved when others bow out of the race. Who knows, you might at some future time have occasion to interact professionally with one of the organizations with which you sought employment. How embarrassing it would be to have someone remember you as the candidate who failed to notify them that you were taking a job elsewhere!

In all of your follow-up communications, keep good notes of whom you spoke with, when you called, and any instructions that were given about return communications. This will prevent any misunderstandings and provide you with good records of what has transpired.

Job Offer Considerations

For many recent college graduates, the thrill of their first job and, for some, the most substantial regular income they have ever earned seems an excess of good fortune coming at once. To question that first income or to be critical in any way of the conditions of employment at the time of the initial offer seems like looking a gift horse in the mouth. It doesn't seem to occur to many new hires even to attempt to negotiate any aspect of their first job. And, as many employers who deal with entry-level jobs for recent college graduates will readily confirm, the reality is that there simply isn't much movement in salary available to these new college recruits. The entry-level hire generally does not have an employment track record on a professional level to provide any leverage for negotiation. Real negotiations on salary, benefits, retirement provisions, and so forth come to those with significant employment records at higher income levels.

Of course, the job offer is more than just money. It can be composed of geographic assignment, duties and responsibilities, training, benefits, health and medical insurance, educational assistance, car allowance or company vehicle, and a host of other items. All of this is generally detailed in the formal letter that presents the final job offer. In most cases this is a follow-up to a personal phone call from the employer representative who has been principally responsible for your hiring process.

That initial telephone offer is certainly binding as a verbal agreement, but most firms follow up with a detailed letter outlining the most significant parts of your employment contract. You may, of course, choose to respond immediately at the time of the telephone offer (which would be considered a binding oral contract), but you will also be required to formally answer the letter of offer with a letter of acceptance, restating the salient elements of the employer's description of your position, salary, and benefits. This ensures that both parties are clear on the terms and conditions of employment and remuneration and any other outstanding aspects of the job offer.

Is This the Job You Want?

Most new employees will respond affirmatively in writing, glad to be in the position to accept employment. If you've worked hard to get the offer and the job market is tight, other offers may not be in sight, so you will say, "Yes, I accept!" What is important here is that the job offer you accept be one that does fit your particular needs, values, and interests as you've outlined them in your self-assessment process. Moreover, it should be a job that will not only use your skills and education but also challenge you to develop new skills and talents.

Jobs are sometimes accepted too hastily, for the wrong reasons, and without proper scrutiny by the applicant. For example, an individual might readily accept a sales job only to find the continual rejection by potential clients unendurable. An office worker might realize within weeks the constraints of a desk job and yearn for more activity. Employment is an important part of our lives. It is, for most of our adult lives, our most continuous productive activity. We want to make good choices based on the right criteria.

If you have a low tolerance for risk, a job based on commission will certainly be very anxiety-provoking. If being near your family is important, issues of relocation could present a decision crisis for you. If you're an adventurous person, a job with frequent travel would provide needed excitement and be very desirable. The importance of income, the need to continue your education, your personal health situation—all of these have an impact on whether the job you are considering will ultimately meet your needs. Unless you've spent some time understanding and thinking about these issues, it will be difficult to evaluate offers you do receive.

More important, if you make a decision that you cannot tolerate and feel you must leave that job, you will then have both unemployment and self-esteem issues to contend with. These will combine to make the next job search tough going, indeed. So make your acceptance a carefully considered decision.

Negotiate Your Offer

It may be that there is some aspect of your job offer that is not particularly attractive to you. Perhaps there is no relocation allotment to help you move your possessions, and this presents some financial hardship for you. It may be that the health insurance is less than you had hoped. Your initial assignment may be different from what you expected, either in its location or in the duties and responsibilities that comprise it. Or it may simply be that the salary is less than you anticipated. Other considerations may be your official starting date of employment, vacation time, evening hours, dates of training programs or schools, and other concerns.

If you are considering not accepting the job because of some item or items in the job offer "package" that do not meet your needs, you should know that most employers emphatically wish that you would bring that issue to their attention. It may be that the employer can alter it to make the offer more agreeable for you. In some cases it cannot be changed. In any event the employer would generally like to have the opportunity to try to remedy a difficulty rather than risk losing a good potential employee over an issue that might have been resolved. After all, they have spent time and funds in securing your services, and they certainly deserve an opportunity to resolve any possible differences.

Honesty is the best approach in discussing any objections or uneasiness you might have over the employer's offer. Having received your formal offer in writing, contact your employer representative and indicate your particular dissatisfaction in a straightforward manner. For example, you might explain that while you are very interested in being employed by this organization, the salary (or any other benefit) is less than you have determined you require. State the terms you need, and listen to the response. You may be asked to put this in writing, or you may be asked to hold off until the firm can decide on a response. If you are dealing with a senior representative of the organization, one who has been involved in hiring for some time, you may get an immediate response or a solid indication of possible outcomes.

Perhaps the issue is one of relocation. Your initial assignment is in the Midwest, and because you had indicated a strong West Coast preference, you are surprised at the actual assignment. You might simply indicate that while you understand the need for the company to assign you based on its needs, you are disappointed and had hoped to be placed on the West Coast. You could inquire if that were still possible and, if not, would it be reasonable to expect a West Coast relocation in the future.

If your request is presented in a reasonable way, most employers will not see this as jeopardizing your offer. If they can agree to your proposal, they will. If not, they will simply tell you so, and you may choose to continue your candidacy with them or remove yourself from consideration. The choice will be up to you.

Some firms will adjust benefits within their parameters to meet the candidate's need if at all possible. If a candidate requires a relocation cost allowance, he or she may be asked to forgo tuition benefits for the first year to accomplish this adjustment. An increase in life insurance may be adjusted by some other benefit trade-off; perhaps a family dental plan is not needed. In these decisions you are called upon, sometimes under time pressure, to know how you value these issues and how important each is to you.

Many employers find they are more comfortable negotiating for candidates who have unique qualifications or who bring especially needed expertise to the organization. Employers hiring large numbers of entry-level college graduates may be far more reluctant to accommodate any changes in offer conditions. They are well supplied with candidates with similar education and experience so that if rejected by one candidate, they can draw new candidates from an ample labor pool.

Compare Offers

The condition of the economy, the job seeker's academic major and particular geographic job market, and individual needs and demands for certain employment conditions may not provide more than one job offer at a time. Some job seekers may feel that no reasonable offer should go unaccepted for the simple fear there won't be another.

In a tough job market, or if the job you seek is not widely available, or when your job search goes on too long and becomes difficult to sustain financially and emotionally, it may be necessary to accept an inferior offer. The alternative is continued unemployment. Even here, when you feel you don't have a choice, you can at least understand that in accepting this particular offer, there may be limitations and conditions you don't appreciate. At the time of acceptance, there were no other alternatives, but you can begin to use that position to gain the experience and talent to move toward a more attractive position.

Sometimes, however, more than one offer is received, and the candidate has the luxury of choice. If the job seeker knows what he or she wants and has done the necessary self-assessment honestly and thoroughly, it may be clear that one of the offers conforms more closely to those expressed wants and needs.

However, if, as so often happens, the offers are similar in terms of conditions and salary, the question then becomes which organization might provide the necessary climate, opportunities, and advantages for your professional development and growth. This is the time when solid employer research and astute questioning during the interviews really pay off. How much did you learn about the employer through your own research and skillful questioning? When the interviewer asked during the interview "Do you have any questions?" did you ask the kinds of questions that would help resolve a choice between one organization and another? Just as an employer must decide among numerous applicants, so must the applicant learn to assess the potential employer. Both are partners in the job search.

Reneging on an Offer

An especially disturbing occurrence for employers and career counseling professionals is when a job seeker formally (either orally or by written contract) accepts employment with one organization and later reneges on the agreement and goes with another employer.

There are all kinds of rationalizations offered for this unethical behavior. None of them satisfies. The sad irony is that what the job seeker is willing to do to the employer—make a promise and then break it—he or she would be outraged to have done to him- or herself: have the job offer pulled. It is a very bad way to begin a career. It suggests the individual has not taken the time to do the necessary self-assessment and self-awareness exercises to think and judge critically. The new offer taken may, in fact, be no better or worse than the one refused. You should be aware that there have been incidents of legal action following job candidates' reneging on an offer. This adds a very sour note to what should be a harmonious beginning of a lifelong adventure.

PART TWO

THE CAREER PATHS

5

Choose Your Career Path

Economists study the ways society distributes scarce resources such as land, labor, raw materials, and machinery to produce goods and services. They conduct research, collect and analyze data, monitor economic trends, and develop forecasts. They research issues such as energy costs, inflation, interest rates, imports, and employment levels.

Most economists are concerned with practical applications of economic policy in a particular area. They use their understanding of economic relationships to advise businesses and other organizations, including insurance companies, banks, securities firms, industry and trade associations, labor unions, and government agencies.

Economists use mathematical models to develop programs predicting answers to questions such as the nature and length of business cycles, the effects of a specific rate of inflation on the economy, or the effects of tax legislation on unemployment levels. Economists devise methods and procedures for obtaining the data they need. For example, they may use sampling techniques to conduct surveys and various mathematical modeling techniques to develop forecasts.

Preparing reports on research results is an important component of economists' jobs. They must review and analyze relevant data, prepare applicable tables and charts, and present the results in clear, concise language that can be understood by laypeople. Presenting economic and statistical concepts in meaningful ways is particularly important for economists whose research is directed toward setting policies for their organizations.

Working Conditions

Economists usually have structured work schedules. They often work alone, writing reports, preparing statistical charts, and using computers, but they may also be an integral part of a research team. Most work under pressure of deadlines and tight schedules, and sometimes they must work overtime. Their routine may be interrupted by special requests for data and by travel for meetings or conferences.

Possible Job Titles

Economics plays important roles in all kinds of fields, so it can be hard to picture what the "average" economics major does day to day after graduation. Take a look at the following list of job titles, and you'll be amazed at how diverse their positions are. What's more, many of these titles apply to both the private and public sectors. Some jobs, such as college teaching, require formal education or training beyond a bachelor's degree.

Banking and Financial Services

Accountant
Auditor
Bank examiner
Bank manager
Bank research analyst
Bond trader
Commercial credit analyst
Commodities broker/
   stockbroker
Commodity analyst
Consumer credit manager
Credit accounting coordinator
Database administrator
Economic forecaster
Economist
Estate planner
Financial adviser
Financial aid director
Foundation administrator
Loan counselor
Loan officer
Pension funds administrator
Portfolio administrator
Purser
Securities analyst
Securities salesperson/broker
Tax economist

Business

Business manager
Compensation/benefits
   administrator
Consumer affairs director
Contract administrator
Cost analyst
Customer account representative
Database administrator
Efficiency expert
Financial economist
Forecaster

Human resources administrator
Industrial economist
Industrial/institutional buyer
Industrial traffic manager
International trade specialist
Management consultant/analyst
Management trainee
Manufacturer's representative
Market analyst
Property manager
Purchasing agent
Real estate agent/broker
Researcher
Retail manager
Sales representative
Service representative
Systems evaluator
Technical representative
Wage and salary administrator

Communications
Marketing manager
Marketing research analyst
Publicity specialist
Public relations representative

Consulting
Consultant

Energy
Economic geologist

Government
Budget officer
Cost analyst
Database administrator
Elected official
Foreign service officer
Foreign trade analyst
Government administrator
Information scientist

Intelligence agent
International trade specialist
Labor economist
Lobbyist
Political campaign organizer
Public administrator/manager
Public utilities manager
Regional/urban planner
Social Security administrator
Tax administrator
Tax examiner/collector/revenue
    agent
Transportation specialist
Treasury management specialist
Urban/regional planner

Health Care
Health care administrator
Health policy planner

Human Services
Corporate trainer
Industrial relations specialist
Labor relations specialist
Personnel manager
Recruiter

Insurance
Actuary
Benefits analyst
Claims adjuster
Database administrator
Demographer
Populations studies analyst
Sales representative
Statistician
Underwriter

Law
Attorney
Judge

Legal assistant
Litigation analyst
Paralegal

Marketing
Database administrator
Market interviewer
Market research analyst
Market research statistician
Marketing manager
Public relations specialist

Teaching
Research assistant
Secondary school teacher
University/college professor

Writing
Editor
Financial reporter
Foreign correspondent
Journalist/columnist
Technical writer

This list is not exhaustive, and through your own research, undoubtedly you will be able to add to the list substantially.

The Career Paths

What college student doesn't hope to find a great job upon graduation? With four years of study and careful planning throughout your college program, and in some cases graduate study, there is no reason why, as an economics major, you shouldn't step into a good job. There are a lot of choices, however, as you've seen from the list of job titles. This book aims to help you narrow them down and find the career path that best suits your education, interests, and skills.

We will identify and explore five main paths. However, your options are not limited to these five. The following section discusses additional fields that economics majors regularly enter.

1. Government
2. Marketing
3. Human resources
4. Banking, finance, and investment
5. Teaching

Additional Paths

The five career paths covered in the following chapters are only some of the many paths that economics majors regularly pursue. About one-third of all economists are employed in private industry. They work for manufacturing firms, insurance companies, transportation companies, economic research firms, and management consulting firms. But economics majors have plenty of other options.

Actuarial Careers

Actuaries answer questions about future risk, make pricing decisions, and formulate investment strategies. Some of them design insurance, financial, and pension plans and ensure that they remain financially sound. Most actuaries specialize in life, health, or property and casualty insurance; others specialize in pension plans.

Actuaries assemble and analyze data to estimate probabilities of death, sickness, injury, disability, retirement income level, property loss, or return on investment. They use this information to estimate how much an insurance company will have to pay out in claims or to make other business decisions. For example, actuaries might calculate the expected amount in claims due to automobile accidents, which can vary depending on the insured's age, gender, driving history, type of car, and other factors. Actuaries ensure that the price charged for such insurance, or premium, will enable the company to cover claims and expenses that it incurs. Finally, this premium must generate a profit while staying competitive with other insurance companies. The actuary calculates premium rates and determines policy contract provisions for each type of insurance offered.

To perform their duties effectively, actuaries must remain informed about general economic and social trends and legislation, as well as developments in health, business, finance, and economics that might affect insurance or investment practices. Using their broad knowledge of business and mathematics, actuaries may work in investment, risk classification, or pension planning.

Careers in Private Research and Consulting Firms

Many private research and development (R&D) firms, consulting firms, and think tanks hire economists. These firms specialize in a wide variety of economic applications. Some of the areas covered by these firms include

Cost-benefit analysis
Econometric analysis for firms and government agencies
Environmental studies
Forensic economics (estimating the value of lost income as a result of wrongful injury or death)
International economics
Market research

Higher-level positions in these firms often require a graduate degree in economics. However, a bachelor's degree is often enough to get in the door as a research assistant.

Health Care Management Careers

Health care spending, both public and private, accounts for about 15 percent of the gross domestic product, a mammoth portion. The industry must find ways to streamline its delivery of care while maintaining quality, complying with regulations, and struggling to turn a profit—undoubtedly good economists have a role to play.

Hospitals are continually growing larger through mergers and consolidation. Like other businesses, they need good management to keep them running smoothly, especially during such tumultuous times The title health services manager encompasses individuals in many different positions who plan, organize, coordinate, and supervise the delivery of health care. Health services managers include both generalists (administrators who manage or help to manage an entire facility or system) and health specialists (managers in charge of specific clinical departments or services found only in the health industry).

The structure and financing of health care is changing rapidly. Future health services managers must be prepared to deal with evolving integrated health care delivery systems, restructuring of work, and ongoing technological innovations.

Health services managers are called upon to improve efficiency in all health care facilities. More than ever, health services managers work in integrated organizations in which they must optimize efficiency of a variety of interrelated services, ranging from inpatient care to outpatient follow-up care.

The chief executive officer (CEO) and other C-level administrators without specific titles are health care generalists. They set the overall direction of the organization, concentrating on such areas as community outreach, planning, marketing, human resources, finance, and regulatory compliance. Their range of knowledge is broad, including understanding developments in the clinical departments as well as in the business arena.

Insurance Careers

Insurance companies protect individuals and organizations from financial loss by assuming billions of dollars in risks each year. In addition to actuaries, economics majors can become underwriters, who identify and analyze the risks of loss from policyholders, establish appropriate premium rates, and write policies that cover that risk. An insurance company may lose business to competitors if the underwriter appraises risks too conservatively, or it may have to pay more claims if the appraisals are too liberal. Insurance companies are in a technological race to automate as much of the risk-assessment process as possible in order to lower their cost per transaction, so rules-based decision-making software, such as CleverPath™'s Aion line, can process most insurance applications. In most offices, this leaves only a small percentage of applications and renewals for underwriters to review—the most complex scenarios. The underwriters can then recommend acceptance or denial of the risk or adjust the premium rate to reflect the risk.

Most underwriters specialize in one of three major categories of insurance—life, property and casualty, or health. They further specialize in group or individual policies. Property and casualty underwriters often specialize by type of risk insured, such as fire, homeowners', automobile, marine, property, liability, or workers' compensation. In cases where casualty companies insure in a single "package" policy, covering various types of risks, the underwriter must be familiar with different lines of insurance. Some underwriters, called commercial account underwriters, handle business insurance exclusively. They often evaluate a firm's entire operation in appraising its application for insurance.

Careers in Labor and Industrial Relations

Economics majors working in the field of labor and industrial relations are responsible for engaging in contract negotiations, processing labor grievances, and dealing with day-to-day labor-management disputes. (This career path is covered with human resource management careers in Chapter 8.)

Law Careers

Many economics majors use their degrees as stepping stones to attend law school and embark on law careers. Law schools report that most students who enter law school have two conspicuous deficiencies: (1) the inability to write and/or speak clearly and correctly and (2) the inability to think critically and make valid analytical comparisons and differentiations. Economics is perhaps one of the best disciplines in which students can develop analytical thought processes with precision and exactness. Law schools are primarily interested in students who possess strong analytical and communication skills and have solid liberal arts backgrounds. Earning a degree in economics is an excellent starting point. The critical thinking and logic required to earn an economics degree generally stand econ majors in good stead when it comes time to take the LSAT. Past studies have shown that they have among the highest median LSAT scores when compared by major.

Public Utilities Careers

Public utilities have employed economists for a long time. They are called upon to forecast demand, assess supply, and analyze and interpret industry regulations. With broad new federal regulations and multistate mergers requiring a careful look at policies and practices, economists should be even more in demand. Public utility economists perform a variety of functions, including

Cost analysis
Demand forecasting
Demand-side management
Market analysis
Technology assessment

In addition, economists develop and defend the rate structures for public utilities.

Transportation Careers

Transportation companies and governments hire graduates who have studied economics and transportation management. Positions might include

Dock supervision
Inventory control
Planning and management of urban and rural transportation systems
Policy analysis
Rate determination
Route development
Scheduling
Transport service marketing
Warehouse and materials management

With a little bit of guidance and creativity, you should be able to make a case for your economics degree in any area you wish to enter.

Employment Patterns

Private industry, particularly economic and marketing research firms, management consulting firms, banks, securities and commodities brokers, and computer and data-processing companies, employ about three out of four salaried economists. The remainder works at a wide range of government agencies, primarily in state governments. The Departments of Labor, Agriculture, and Commerce are the largest federal employers of economists.

A number of economists combine full-time jobs in government, academia, or business with part-time or consulting work in another setting.

Employment of economists is concentrated in large cities. Some economists work abroad for companies with major international operations, for U.S. government agencies such as the Foreign Service, and for international organizations such as the World Bank, International Monetary Fund (IMF), and the United Nations.

In addition to the jobs just described, many economists hold faculty positions at colleges and universities. Economics faculty have flexible work schedules and may divide their time among teaching, research, consulting, and administration.

Preparing for the Work

Graduate training is required for most private-sector economists' jobs and for advancement to more responsible positions. Candidates who hold master's degrees in economics have much better employment prospects than those with only bachelor's degrees.

Economics includes many specialties at the graduate level, such as advanced economic theory, econometrics, international economics, and labor economics. Students should select graduate schools strong in specialties in which the students are interested. Some schools help graduate students find internships or part-time employment in government agencies, economic consulting firms, financial institutions, or marketing research firms before graduation.

In the federal government, candidates for entry-level economist positions must have bachelor's degrees with a minimum of twenty-one semester hours of economics and three hours of statistics, accounting, or calculus. Competition is keen for positions that require only bachelor's degrees, however. You'll enhance your prospects with a strong undergraduate academic performance and postgraduate education.

For a job as an instructor in many junior and some community colleges, a master's degree is the minimum requirement. In most colleges and universities, however, a Ph.D. is necessary for appointment as an instructor. A Ph.D. and numerous publications in academic journals are required for a professorship, tenure, and promotion.

Whether working in government, industry, research, marketing, or consulting, economists who have graduate degrees usually qualify for more responsible research and administrative positions. A Ph.D. is necessary for top economist positions in many organizations. Many corporate executives and government employees have strong backgrounds in economics or marketing.

A bachelor's degree with a major in economics or marketing is generally not sufficient to obtain a position as an economist, but it is excellent preparation for many entry-level positions as a research assistant, administrative or management trainee, marketing interviewer, or numerous professional sales jobs.

Economics majors can choose from a variety of courses, ranging from those that are intensely mathematical, such as microeconomics, macroeconomics, and econometrics, to more philosophical courses, such as the history of economic thought. Because of the importance of quantitative skills to economists, courses in mathematics, statistics, econometrics, sampling theory and survey design, and computer science are extremely helpful.

Aspiring economists should gain experience gathering and analyzing data, conducting interviews or surveys, and writing reports on their findings while in college. Much of your entry-level work might involve these same skills, so the early experience can prove invaluable when it comes time to look for work.

With experience, economists eventually are assigned their own research projects. Those considering careers as economists should have a great attention to detail because much time is spent on data analysis. Patience and persistence are necessary qualities, since economists must spend long hours on independent study and problem solving. Economists also must be able to present their findings, both verbally and in writing, in a clear, meaningful manner.

Graduate Study

Because so many professional economics positions require advanced degrees, economics majors use their bachelor's degrees as stepping stones and go on to postgraduate study in areas such as economics, applied mathematics and statistics, public policy, labor relations, law, marketing, international affairs, banking, and public policy. Those preparing for academic careers at the university level usually go on to earn doctoral degrees.

Career Outlook

Though applicable to a large number of disciplines, economics is an elite field. Employment opportunities should increase through 2014, but they will grow more slowly than the job market as a whole. The good news is that because economics has so many applications, graduates are likely to find good work in related fields—perhaps as financial analysts, market analysts, public policy consultants, or research assistants. This is especially promising for those with bachelor's degrees given that pure economics positions generally require advanced degrees. They can take advantage of their economic knowledge by conducting research, developing surveys, or analyzing data. Bachelor's degree holders with good quantitative skills and a strong background in mathematics, statistics, survey design, and computer science also might find jobs with private firms as researchers; some may work in government. Others could get into teaching; the demand for secondary-school economics teachers will become stronger as knowledge of economics gains importance in the Information Age.

A master's degree or Ph.D. is a prerequisite for virtually any specialty within the economics field, along with a strong background in economic theory, mathematics, statistics, and econometrics. Good communicators who are skilled in quantitative techniques and their application to economic modeling and forecasting should have the best job opportunities. The fastest employment growth will be in private industry, especially in management, scientific, and technical consulting services. Rising demand for economic analysis in virtually every industry should stem from the growing complexity of the global economy, the effects of competition on businesses, and increased reliance on quantitative methods for analyzing and forecasting business, sales, and other economic trends. Some corporations choose to hire consultants to fill these needs rather than keeping an economist on staff, which should result in more economists working in consulting services. Overall, few new jobs are expected in government, but the need to replace experienced workers who transfer to other occupations or who retire or otherwise leave the labor force will lead to job openings for economists across all industries in which they are employed. Nevertheless, as in other disciplines, the competition for jobs among Ph.D.s will be keen.

Salaries

A 2005 survey by the National Association of Colleges and Employers shows that graduates with bachelor's degrees in economics fall in the middle of the pack when their earning power is compared with that of graduates from other disciplines. Those in economics averaged $41,994 annually, below engineering and computer science majors but above liberal arts majors and business majors.

Average Salaries by Major*

Chemical engineering	$53,639
Electrical/electronics engineering	$51,773
Computer science	$50,664
Mechanical engineering	$50,175
Management information systems	$43,653
Accounting	$42,940
Economics/finance	$41,994
Business administration/management	$39,480
Marketing/marketing management	$36,409
Liberal arts & sciences/general studies	$32,725
History	$31,739
Psychology	$30,073

*Bachelor's degree level.
Source: NACE Fall 2005 Salary Survey

This is merely a starting point, however. The vast majority of economists hold advanced degrees, and compensation rises accordingly. The median base salary for members of the National Association for Business Economics is nearly $100,000. Figures drawn from the association's annual salary survey reveal the earning potential available to economists with master's and doctoral degrees:

Median Starting Salary by Degree, 2005

Bachelor's	$42,362
Master's	$52,451
Ph.D.	$75,161

Median Annual Salary by Degree, 2005

Bachelor's	$80,846
Master's	$89,669
Ph.D.	$116,301

Source: National Association for Business Economics.

The highest-paid business economists work in the securities and investment industry. The lowest pay is in government and nonprofit research. The starting salary for federal government economists with bachelor's degrees is about $24,667; a graduate with a superior academic record might begin at $30,567. Earning a postgraduate degree makes a measurable difference. Positions that require a master's start at an average of $37,390, and those needing a Ph.D. begin at about $45,239 right out of school. With some work experience and an advanced degree, the average government economist starts at about $54,221. The average annual salary for economists employed by the federal government was $89,441 in 2005. Of course, salaries vary by region and city size. Check out websites such as Salary.com to compare salaries by region.

Resources

See Appendix A, "Professional Associations," and Appendix B, "Web Resources," for job-search tools, further research and statistics, and industry news.

Path 1: Government

The public sector represents a huge employment opportunity for economists—counting federal, state, and local entities, government employs 58 percent of all economists in the United States.

Economists working in government agencies fill a variety of roles and work in almost every area of government. They may assess economic conditions in the United States or abroad to estimate the economic effects of specific changes in legislation or public policy. Or they may study issues such as how the dollar's fluctuation against foreign currencies affects import and export levels.

In the United States, the largest federal employers of economists are the Departments of Labor, Agriculture, and State. Some economists in the U.S. Department of Commerce study production, distribution, and consumption of commodities produced overseas, while economists in the Bureau of Labor Statistics analyze data on the domestic economy: prices, wages, employment, productivity, and safety and health. Economists in state or local government might weigh the types and rates of crime committed against available prison space, or research the effects of public health issues on school attendance.

Possible Government Settings

Economists work for myriad government agencies, departments, and programs. In the United States, those include

Bureau of Labor Statistics
Census Bureau
Congressional Budget Office
Consumer Product Safety Commission

Department of Agriculture
Department of Commerce
Department of Energy
Department of Health and Human Services
Department of Housing and Urban Development
Department of the Interior
Department of Labor
Department of State
Department of the Treasury
Environmental Protection Agency
Federal Reserve Board
National Credit Union Administration
National Labor Relations Board
Office of the Comptroller of the Currency
Office of Management and Budget
Peace Corps
Pension Benefit Guaranty Corporation
Securities and Exchange Commission
Selective Service System
Small Business Administration
Social Security Administration
United States Information Agency
United States International Development Cooperation Agency
United States International Trade Commission

Canada also has a large number of agencies, departments, and programs that employ economists, including

Agriculture and Agri-Food Canada
Bank of Canada
Business Development Bank of Canada
Canada Border Services Agency
Canada Deposit Insurance Corporation
Canada Mortgage and Housing Corporation
Canada Pension Plan Investment Board
Canada Revenue Agency
Canadian Centre for Occupational Health and Safety
Canadian Environmental Assessment Agency
Canadian International Development Agency
Department of Finance Canada
Environment Canada
Fisheries and Oceans Canada

Foreign Affairs Canada
Health Canada
Human Resources and Skills Development Canada
Industry Canada
International Trade Canada
National Defence
National Research Council Canada
Statistics Canada

This list is by no means exhaustive. Through your own investigation, you will probably be able to add many more agencies and departments to the list.

Possible Job Titles

The U.S. government has assigned a number of job titles based on college majors. The following job titles fall into the realm of employment for which an economics major could be qualified. Related majors and their associated job titles are also included here. You will find that some jobs are appropriate for more than one major.

Major: Economics
Actuary
Budget analyst
Contract specialist
Economist
Financial analyst
Financial institution examiner
General Accounting Office (GAO) evaluator
Loan specialist
Trade specialist
Transportation industrial analyst

Major: Employee/Labor Relations
Contractor industrial relations specialist
Employee-relations specialist
Hearing and appeals specialist
Labor/management relations examiner
Labor relations specialist
Mediator
Salary and wage administrator
Workers compensation claims examiner

Major: Finance
Appraiser
Assessor
Budget analyst
Financial administrator
Financial analyst
Financial institution examiner
Securities compliance examiner
Tax examiner
Trade specialist

Major: Hospital Administration
Administrative officer
General health scientist
Health system administrator
Health system specialist
Miscellaneous administration and programs specialist
Public health programs specialist

Major: Human Resource Management
Apprenticeship and training representative
Employee development specialist
Equal employment opportunity specialist
Military personnel management specialist
Personnel manager
Position classification specialist

Major: Insurance
Crop insurance administrator
Miscellaneous administration and programs specialist
Program analyst
Social insurance administrator
Social insurance claims examiner
Unemployment insurance specialist

Major: International Relations
Foreign affairs specialist
Foreign agriculture affairs specialist
Intelligence specialist
International relations worker
Language specialist

Public affairs specialist
Trade specialist

Major: Law

Administrative law judge
Attorney
General Accounting Office (GAO) evaluator
Hearing and appeals specialist
Legal instruments examiner
Paralegal specialist
Patent attorney
Tax law specialist

Major: Marketing

Agriculture marketing specialist
Bond sales promotion representative
Business and industry specialist
Contract specialist
Inventory management specialist
Packaging specialist
Property disposal specialist
Supply specialist
Trade specialist

Major: Mathematics

Actuary
Cartographer
Computer science specialist
Mathematical statistician
Mathematician
Operations research analyst
Statistician

Major: Planning, Community or City

Community planner
Realtor

Major: Political Science/Government

Archivist
Budget analyst

General Accounting Office (GAO) evaluator
Foreign affairs specialist
Historian
Miscellaneous administration and programs specialist
Program analyst
Public affairs specialist
Social scientist

Major: Public Administration

Budget analyst
Employee development specialist
Employee relations specialist
General Accounting Office (GAO) evaluator
Housing manager
Management analyst
Manpower development specialist
Miscellaneous administration and programs specialist
Program analyst
Public utilities specialist

Major: Public Relations/Journalism

Contact representative
Foreign affairs specialist
Foreign agriculture affairs specialist
Public affairs specialist

Major: Statistics

Actuary
Computer science specialist
Mathematical statistician
Operations research analyst
Program analyst
Statistician
Transportation industry analyst

Any Major

Administrative officer
Air traffic controller
Civil rights analyst
Claims examiner
Contract administrator

Contract representative
Editor
Environmental protection agent
General investigator
Internal revenue officer
Logistics manager
Management analyst
Paralegal specialist
Personnel occupations officer

Preparing for the Work

Landing a higher-level government position often requires a graduate degree in economics. Graduates with bachelor's degrees are generally hired as research or economics assistants when just starting out. Advancement comes over time.

Students interested in pursuing careers in government service should include the following courses in their undergraduate curriculum: mathematical economics; law and economics; econometrics; economics of regulation; and forecasting. Smart electives to consider are international economics, labor economics, and antitrust and regulation. It is also important to acquire experience with database and statistical software, and strong communications skills are essential.

Finding Your Government Job

The United States and Canada have one primary source each for job-hunting economics majors—and anyone else in search of a government job.

United States
In the United States, the USAJobs website (usajobs.opm.gov), operated by the Office of Personnel Management, makes searching for federal government jobs easy to do. It also covers state and local job listings (see thejobpage. gov/statelocal.asp). You can set up an account on the site, post your resume, and, in many cases, apply for jobs directly with the hiring agency. Try searching under a variety of categories in the "Basic Search" function. You might find relevant openings under "Accounting, Budget and Finance," "Business, Industry and Procurement," "Mathematics and Statistics," and other headings. You can also search by agency as well as "series number," the four-digit grouping code used to classify jobs (economist is 0110, but again, appropriate jobs could fall under a variety of codes, so don't search too narrowly).

The government requires that all "competitive civil service jobs," those subject to congressional hiring laws, be listed on the site. By setting up an account on USAJobs, job seekers can have relevant openings e-mailed to them. The system also has a twenty-four-hour phone component that users can call to find out about vacancies: (703) 724-1850; TDD (978) 461-8404.

Canada

The Public Service Commission of Canada runs a similar website, Jobs.gc. ca (jobs-emplois.gc.ca). Likes USAJobs, Jobs.gc.ca does not list every position open in government—some are not open to the public and are posted only on the government's intranet. (In addition, many agencies are not subject to the Public Service Employment Act and are not required to post jobs to this central clearinghouse site. These agencies recruit independently and post openings on their own websites. For a list of those agencies, go to jobs-emplois.gc.ca/menu/useful-info_e.htm.) However, nearly all job openings are on the site, and job seekers can apply directly online in many cases.

Job listings here are divided between jobs open to the general public and specialized recruitment programs, which include postsecondary recruitment, a research affiliate program, and a co-op/internship program. Current students nearing graduation will be especially interested in the postsecondary recruitment listings, which contain entry-level jobs intended for undergraduate students coming right out of school. You can also call the automated twenty-four-hour Infotel job line at (800) 645-5605 to listen to job listings, though the website contains more complete information and an easier application process.

Federal Employment Overseas

The federal government has technical, administrative, and supervisory employment opportunities overseas. These positions are usually in the competitive federal service and, as vacancies occur, are typically filled by transferring career federal employees from the United States. Only when federal employees are not available for transfer overseas and qualified U.S. citizens cannot be recruited locally are these vacancies filled through the open examination process. For opportunities overseas, see detailed information at usajobs.opm.gov/EI10.asp.

Individuals may also apply directly to federal agencies for excepted service positions such as attaché office clerk-translator, translator, interpreter, and Foreign Service, Department of State positions.

Federal employers of individuals overseas include but are not limited to

Agency for International Development
Department of Agriculture
Department of the Army
Department of the Air Force
Department of Commerce
Department of Defense
Department of the Navy
Department of State
Peace Corps
U.S. Information Agency

Qualifications for U.S. Government Jobs Overseas

Generally, the qualification requirements for overseas jobs are the same as those established for positions within the United States. Applicants may, however, be required to meet certain additional or higher standards. For example, a foreign language capability, while not required in all federal jobs overseas, would obviously be a valuable skill.

Student Programs with the Federal Government

The federal government is interested in finding people from diverse backgrounds who have the skills needed to meet its future employment needs. While some federal agencies have developed independent programs and seek students in specific majors, such as economics, there are also a variety of internships, work-study opportunities, cooperative education appointments, and summer programs that can lead to hiring in all federal agencies. Full information is available at usajobs.opm.gov/EI-13.asp. Students can also find temporary and long-term employment through the website studentjobs.gov.

Government Salaries

The U.S. government ranks white-collar jobs using levels on the "general schedule" (GS-1 through GS-15) according to the job's level of difficulty and responsibility. See Exhibit 6.1. Within each grade, there are ten increments through which an employee advances—and receives a corresponding pay increase. The general schedule as of 2006 follows below. The GS grade is

Exhibit 6.1
U.S. GOVERNMENT'S GENERAL SCHEDULE FOR SALARIES, 2006*

Grade	Step 1	Step 2	Step 3	Step 4	Step 5	Step 6	Step 7	Step 8	Step 9	Step 10
GS-1	16,352	16,898	17,442	17,983	18,527	18,847	19,383	19,925	19,947	20,450
GS-2	18,385	18,822	19,431	19,947	20,169	20,762	21,355	21,948	22,541	23,134
GS-3	20,060	20,729	21,398	22,067	22,736	23,405	24,074	24,743	25,412	26,081
GS-4	22,519	23,270	24,021	24,772	25,523	26,274	27,025	27,776	28,527	29,278
GS-5	25,195	26,035	26,875	27,715	28,555	29,395	30,235	31,075	31,915	32,755
GS-6	28,085	29,021	29,957	30,893	31,829	32,765	33,701	34,637	35,573	36,509
GS-7	31,209	32,249	33,289	34,329	35,369	36,409	37,449	38,489	39,529	40,569
GS-8	34,563	35,715	36,867	38,019	39,171	40,323	41,475	42,627	43,779	44,931
GS-9	38,175	39,448	40,721	41,994	43,267	44,540	45,813	47,086	48,359	49,632
GS-10	42,040	43,441	44,842	46,243	47,644	49,045	50,446	51,847	53,248	54,649
GS-11	46,189	47,729	49,269	50,809	52,349	53,889	55,429	56,969	58,509	60,049
GS-12	55,360	57,205	59,050	60,895	62,740	64,585	66,430	68,275	70,120	71,965
GS-13	65,832	68,026	70,220	72,414	74,608	76,802	78,996	81,190	83,384	85,578
GS-14	77,793	80,386	82,979	85,572	88,165	90,758	93,351	95,944	98,537	101,130
GS-15	91,507	94,557	97,607	100,657	103,707	106,757	109,807	112,857	115,907	118,957

*Annual salaries given in U.S. dollars.

listed in the left-hand column; numbers in the top row indicate steps within each grade.

This schedule indicates only the baseline pay for each level. GS pay is adjusted geographically, and the majority of jobs pay a higher salary than those listed here. (You can download locality pay tables and a GS schedule with hourly pay rates at opm.gov/flsa/oca/06tables/indexGS.asp.) When locality payments are included, pay rates in the continental United States are as much as 12 percent higher. Pay rates outside the continental United States are up to 25 percent higher. Also, certain hard-to-fill jobs, usually in the scientific, technical, and medical fields, may have higher starting salaries. Exact pay information can be found on position vacancy announcements.

The Treasury Board of Canada takes a more customized approach to pay for public service employees. See tbs-sct.gc.ca/pubs_pol/hrpubs/RatesofPay/Ra97_e.asp for current information on Canadian government pay scales.

Sample Job Ads

To get an idea of the types of positions available and the salaries they command, examine the sample job announcements in Exhibits 6.2 through 6.4.

Exhibit 6.2
SAMPLE JOB ANNOUNCEMENT

Position: Budget Analyst
Hiring Agency: Immigration and Customs Enforcement
Series & Grade: GS-0560-07
Salary: $35,452 to $46,088 USD per year
Promotion Potential: GS-13
Duty Location: Washington, DC
Position Information: Full-time career/career conditional

This position supports our mission to prevent acts of terrorism by targeting the people, money, and materials that support terrorist and criminal activities. Our vision is to be the nation's preeminent law enforcement agency, dedicated to detecting vulnerabilities and preventing violations that threaten national security. Immigration and Customs Enforcement (ICE) was established to combat the criminal and national security threats emergent in a post-9/11 environment.

(continued)

Exhibit 6.2
SAMPLE JOB ANNOUNCEMENT *(continued)*

This position is located in the Department of Homeland Security, Immigration and Customs Enforcement, Office of the Chief Financial Officer. The incumbent performs a variety of budgeting functions involving the formulation, justification, and execution phases of the budget. The incumbent is responsible for a segment of the organization's budget.

A background investigation is required. Drug screening is required. Must be a U.S. citizen.

Duties: As an advanced trainee, increases knowledge, skills, and abilities in various phases of the budget process. Researches regulations and other pertinent directives for answers prior to consulting with the supervisor or a higher-graded employee. Successfully completes required formal and on-the-job training, and demonstrates a progressive ability to independently accomplish assignments. Prepares budget estimates for assigned program areas. Performs routine budget administration duties and analysts functions. Gathers, reviews, verifies and consolidates information and statistical data needed in formulation and presentation of budget requests. Checks and monitors the rate and amount of obligations and expenditures for assigned program areas. Recommends the adjustment of inconsistent totals and entries. Compares projected costs for assigned areas in the budget with prior year expenditures for the same items. Translates the service organization's needs and objectives, by assigned program areas, into budget dollars and the funding actions required to accomplish them. Compiles, analyzes, and summarizes financial and/or budgetary information related to assigned areas of the organization's financial program. Prepares well-researched and logically organized presentations related to work assignments. Relates the needs and accomplishments of the organization to anticipated and/or actual dollar figures in the budget. Prepares summaries of statistical data in budget reports and schedules. Prepares preliminary budget estimates and reviews justifications for reports. Serves as a source of information on specific rules and procedures governing the processing of routine budgetary actions.

Requirements: GS-07: Applicants must meet at least one of the qualification requirements described under A, B, or C below:

(A) Education (undergraduate and/or graduate): A bachelor's degree in any field, plus at least one of the following superior academic achievement provisions: (1)

A GPA of 3.0 or higher on a 4.0 scale for all completed undergraduate courses, or courses completed in the last two years of undergraduate curriculum; (2) A GPA of 3.5 or higher on a 4.0 scale for the required courses in your major field of study, or required courses in your major completed in the last two years of undergraduate study; (3) Rank in the upper one-third of your class in the college, university, or major subdivision at the time of application; (4) Election to membership in a national scholastic honor society, other than freshman honor societies. OR Graduate education: One full year of graduate level study or a master's or higher degree, e.g., LL.B., J.D., LL.M., Ph.D., etc.

(B) Specialized experience: To qualify at the GS-7 level, you must possess one year of specialized experience that equipped you with the skills needed to perform the job duties. This experience must have been equivalent to at least the GS-5 grade level. Performing a variety of budgeting functions involving the formulation, justification, and execution phases of the budget; gathers, reviews, verifies, and consolidates information and statistical data needed in formulation and presentation of budget requests; checks and monitors the rate and amount of obligations and expenditures for assigned line items and work units; compares projected costs for selected line items in the budget with prior year expenditures for the same items; prepares summaries of statistical data in budget reports and schedules; prepares preliminary budget estimates and reviews justifications for reports.

(C) Combination of graduate education and experience: Less than the full amount of graduate education described in "A" and less than the amount of experience described in "B," but have a combination of the type of graduate education described in "A" and the type of experience described in "B." First determine your total qualifying specialized experience as a percentage of the experience required for this grade level (in this case, one year). Then determine your total number of successfully completed graduate semester hours as a percentage of education required for this grade level (in this case, 18 semester hours, or whatever amount your school has determined to equal one full year). Then add the percentages. The total percentage must equal at least 100 percent to qualify under this provision.

Exhibit 6.3

SAMPLE JOB ANNOUNCEMENT

Position: Regional Economist
Hiring Agency: U.S. Army Corps of Engineers
Series & Grade: GS-0110-1111
Salary: $55,033 to $71,544 USD per year
Duty Location: Los Angeles, California
Position Information: Full-time/permanent position

Challenge yourself—be an Army civilian! Civilian employees serve a vital role in supporting the Army mission. They provide the skills that are not readily available in the military, but crucial to support military operations. The Army integrates the talents and skills of its military and civilian members to form a total Army. Organization: U.S. Army Engineer District, Los Angeles, Planning Division, Economic and Social Analysis Group, Los Angeles, California. Who may apply: Interagency Career Transition Assistance Plan (ICTAP) eligibles, all U.S. citizens.

Duties: Performs economic research and analysis in the preparation of study reports, economic updates, and appendices for water-resources development projects. The incumbent participates in the determination and evaluation of benefits derived from proposed flood control, navigation, and water supply. Assignments are portions of a larger study or complete studies that require application of conventional research procedures. Determines research requirements, plans the sequence of tasks, and arranges schedules for the study process. Determines sources of data, types of benefits involved, study team, and fieldwork requirements. Using computer modeling, analyzes and evaluates data to determine potential damage to flooded areas, quantifies benefits to be derived from proposed improvements, estimates economic impact of the project, and develops alternatives to identify projects of benefit to the federal government. Prepares reports and appendices to document findings, recommendations, benefit areas, etc.

Requirements: Specialized experience: Knowledge of economics and the uses of standard procedures and processes to perform water-resource-related economic studies. Utilizes a variety of resources (maps, personal interviews, physical inventories) to collect pertinent and accurate data for use in economic studies. Researches and analyzes economic data and prepares interpretive reports to assist government officials in making decisions regarding various programs of the federal government. Knowledge of techniques of quantifying, measuring, and understanding economic relations through the use of computers.

Education can be substituted for experience. Review the qualification requirements for specific information. One year of experience in the same or similar work equivalent to at least the next lower grade or level requiring application of the knowledge, skills, and abilities of the position being filled. Only degrees from an accredited college or university recognized by the Department of Education are acceptable to meet positive education requirements or to substitute education for experience.

GS-11: Bachelor's degree directly related to this occupation and one year of experience directly related to this occupation equivalent to the next lower grade level, or three years of progressively higher level graduate education leading to a Ph.D. or equivalent doctoral degree.

Exhibit 6.4

SAMPLE JOB ANNOUNCEMENT

Position: Supervisory Contract Specialist
Hiring Agency: Department of Health and Human Services (National Institutes of Health)
Series & Grade: GS-1102-1414
Salary: $88,369 to $114,882 USD per year
Promotion Potential: GS-14
Duty Location: Bethesda, Maryland
Position Information: Full-time/permanent position

Become a part of the department that touches the lives of every American! At the Department of Health and Human Services, you can give back to your community, state, and country by making a difference in the lives of Americans everywhere. Join HHS and help to make our world healthier, safer, and better for all Americans.

The Office of Research Facilities (ORF), Division of Real Property Acquisition Services (DPRAS), advises the Director, ORF, on acquisition regulations, policies, procedures, and operations for construction and facilities. The Facilities Support Services Contracting Branch (FSSCB) manages the NIH acquisition program for architecture, engineering, and construction services from

(continued)

Exhibit 6.4
SAMPLE JOB ANNOUNCEMENT (continued)

acquisition through negotiation and contract award to contract closeout; serves as the principal advisor to the NIH and expert on regulations, policies, procedures, and processes related to procurement of facilities support; and provides advice, assistance, and training in the areas of facilities support to NIH project officers and NIH Institute and Center (IC) customers.

Duties: The incumbent of this position serves as the Chief, FSSCB and is responsible for directing the activities of the organization and providing leadership to the staff. The Branch Chief is recognized as an expert in those portions of the FAR and HHSAR relevant to the acquisition of the facilities support in research services, and maintains a Certificate of Appointment (Warrant) as a Contracting Officer of the United States. Serves as a contracting officer with unlimited signatory authority for the NIH acquisitions program for facilities support services. The NIH is the principal biomedical research agency of the federal government, with programs involving billions of dollars and affecting millions of people. The acquisition program influences the conduct of research carried out in laboratory and clinical facilities and through grant and contract support throughout the United States and abroad.

Leads and manages the NIH acquisition program for facilities support services from acquisition through negotiation and contract award to contract closeout. Uses knowledge of a variety of contract instruments allowed under such policies as the FAR, HHSAR. Serves as the principal advisor to the NIH, including senior management and program officials.

Directs the full range of contract administration actions required for the NIH acquisition program through a staff of senior contracting specialists. Includes the issuance of contract modifications, negotiation of changes, exercise of options, investigation and resolution of contractor delays, contractor performance appraisal, subcontractor surveillance, disposition of claims, and similar matters.

Has authority for all contractual actions and phases of the NIH acquisition program. Plans, develops, and establishes the contractual strategy for the overall NIH acquisition program. Develops prenegotiation positions, determines the types of contracts and negotiation authority to be used, and prepares justifications.

Manages the evaluation of others, including the orchestration of the technical review. Monitors and evaluates contract performance, negotiates and executes contract changes, resolves postaward issues, and terminates contracts as appropriate. Provides expert advise, assistance, and training in the areas of facilities support contracting to NIH project officers and NIH IC customers. Serves as the principal advisor to the Program Management Office, and represents the ORF, Division Director of Acquisition Services and NIH senior management as the program's contractual authority at conferences and meetings.

Supervises a staff of contracting professionals (GS-12/13 level) and related support specialists who are considered collectively as experts in the acquisitions field. Supervises and directs the operations of the branch by planning and assigning work to staff based on management priorities, employee capabilities, and schedules.

Requirements: Completion of all mandatory training prescribed by the head of the agency including at least four years' experience in contracting or related positions. At least one year of that experience must have been specialized experience at or equivalent to work at the next lower grade level of the position, and must have provided the knowledge, skills, and abilities to perform successfully the work of the position.

AND

A four-year course of study leading to a bachelor's degree that included or was supplemented by at least 24 semester hours in any combination of the following fields: accounting, business, finance, law, contracts, purchasing, economics, industrial management, marketing, quantitative methods or organization and management.

1. Knowledge of government contract laws and general business practices, especially those practices related to the architectural/engineering selection and construction and facilities support contracting.
2. Ability to analyze completed procurement data and recommend solutions.
3. Ability to manage and supervise an organization.
4. Ability to communicate verbally.
5. Ability to communicate in writing.

Foreign Service

A career serving your country overseas can offer excitement, challenge, and even glamour. As a member of the Foreign Service, which is under the jurisdiction of the U.S. Department of State, you can travel the world and at the same time gain the satisfaction of helping other people and representing the interests of your country.

Being a part of the Foreign Service is more than just a job. It is a complete way of life that requires dedication and commitment. If you're smart enough and tough enough to get the job done, the Foreign Service might just be the right place for you. The Foreign Service offers its officers five different career tracks:

1. Management affairs: Management personnel at overseas posts are responsible for hiring foreign national workers, providing office and residential space, ensuring reliable communications with Washington, DC, supervising computer systems, and—of great importance in hostile or unfriendly areas—providing security for the post's personnel and property.

2. Consular affairs: Consular workers must often combine the skills of lawyers, judges, investigators, and social workers. Their duties range from issuing passports and visas to finding a lost child or helping a traveler in trouble.

3. Economic affairs: Economic officers maintain contact with key business and financial leaders in the host country and report to Washington on local economic conditions and their impact on American trade and investment policies. They might work on such sensitive foreign policy issues as the environment or HIV/AIDS, or deal in customary trade agreements and international finance. Whatever their focus, they promote U.S. policies and interests to the rest of the world.

4. Political affairs: Those working in political affairs analyze and report on the political views of the host country. They make contact with labor unions, humanitarian organizations, educators, and cultural leaders.

5. Public diplomacy: As part of the Foreign Service, the United States Information Agency (USIA) promotes U.S. cultural, informational, and public diplomacy programs. An information officer might develop a library open to the public, meet with the press, and oversee English-language training programs for the host country.

Foreign Service officers can be based in Washington, DC, or they can be posted anywhere in the world. They work at embassies, consulates, and other diplomatic missions in major cities and small towns. They help the thousands of Americans traveling and living overseas, issue visas to citizens of other countries wishing to visit the United States, and help our government execute its foreign policies.

The Foreign Service officer accepts direction from the president of the United States and his top appointees. The main goal is to make U.S. policies succeed. He or she is expected to place loyalty over personal opinions and preferences.

Foreign Service workers can experience a glamorous lifestyle, dining with their ambassadors in European palaces and meeting royalty or other heads of state. They can be present at important decision-making sessions and influence world politics and history. But assignments, or postings, can include hardship as well, in environments as hostile as Antarctica and the Middle East. Danger from health hazards, unrest, or war is always possible. In spite of the difficulties, those in the Foreign Service are usually happy with the unique rewards and opportunities.

Training: Although many Foreign Service officers are skilled in political science and history, these days candidates can have knowledge in specialized fields such as the environment, computer science, the fight against AIDS, antidrug efforts, and trade.

Eligibility

Before you can take the Foreign Service written examination, you must be

- At least twenty years old on the date of the exam
- No more than fifty-nine years old
- A citizen of the United States
- Available for worldwide assignment

Applying to the Foreign Service

Foreign Service specialists, who provide technical, support, or administrative services, must fill out application DS-1950 and undergo a preliminary round of vetting. (See careers.state.gov/specialist/join/index.html for details.) Those who meet the Foreign Service's standard will take a written and oral assessment to determine if they have the traits and charisma necessary to do the job. Successful candidates will receive either an immediate conditional offer or, if their assessment scores are not quite high enough, will go on a list of eligible hires for up to two years until openings become available. Specialists work in one of seven areas: administration, construction engineering, information technology, international information and English-language programs, medical and health, office management, or security.

Applicants to become Foreign Service officers undergo a more rigorous selection process:

1. Written examination: This is a daylong multiple-choice test usually given once a year. It measures verbal and numerical reasoning, political and cultural awareness, English-language expression, and knowledge of topics important to the function of the Foreign Service. It's a difficult exam, and many people have to take it more than once before they pass.

2. Oral evaluation: Those who pass the written exam will be invited to participate in an all-day oral assessment. It tests the skills, abilities, knowledge, and personal characteristics necessary to succeed in the Foreign Service. Writing skills are also measured, as well as administrative, problem solving, leadership, and interpersonal skills.

3. Medical clearance: Because many postings have inadequate health care or pose health hazards, candidates for the Foreign Service must meet a high medical standard. Allowances are made, however, for certain handicaps.

4. Background investigation: The Department of State, along with other federal, state, and local agencies, conducts thorough background checks on Foreign Service candidates. They examine employment records, credit histories, repayment of school loans, drug abuse, and criminal records.

For more information on the application process to become a Foreign Service officer, visit careers.state.gov/officer/index.html.

Job Outlook
The Foreign Service exam is not always offered on a yearly basis—the exam is given when there are definite positions to fill. Because competition is keen for all positions, the number of candidates tends to exceed the number of openings. Most openings arise from the need to replace Foreign Service workers who retire or leave the profession for other reasons.

Salaries
The Foreign Service has its own pay scale and system for determining employees' salaries. Pay is similar to other government occupations but more flexible because of the many variables in determining a fair wage: overseas housing, travel, previous income, educational allowances for children, and compensation for "hardship" posts. See careers.state.gov/officer/benefits/index. html#salary for more information.

Close-Up

Get an inside look at the career path of a longtime Foreign Service officer.

Jim Van Laningham, Management Officer
Jim Van Laningham has made the Foreign Service his career for more than fifteen years. He's been posted in Russia in the former Soviet Union, Poland, Morocco, Iraq, and Washington, DC. He became motivated to help improve the image of the United States abroad after reading *The Ugly American* in junior high. He earned a bachelor's in economics and a master's in international business and took the exam right after earning his MBA.

Even with all the information from business school fresh in his mind, a year and a half passed from the time he took the exam until he was accepted. "I was very excited," he says. "They called me up one day and asked if I could be there in less than a month. They wanted an answer right away. My wife and I discussed it and decided to take the plunge." They traveled to Washington, where he worked through a two-month basic orientation course for new officers and underwent six months of language training.

Upon completion of his language training, Van Laningham was assigned to the embassy in Moscow as an economics officer, though today it's almost mandatory that the first tour for Foreign Service officers is as a consular officer, issuing visas to people who want to come to the United States.

On the Job. Administrative officers are responsible for keeping the embassy operating on a day-to-day basis. First thing in the morning, Van Laningham might find a series of cables from Washington waiting that would require him to report on certain information. Depending on the time of the year, he could be involved in renewing leases on houses they were renting to American staff, or help prepare the budget for the embassy, anywhere from a million dollars on up. The budget covers salaries of embassy staff, electricity and other utilities, and procurement of paper and pencils, computers, copy machines, and other office equipment.

Lunch might entail meeting several officers from other embassies, such as Australia, Canada, or Great Britain, to discuss issues. The afternoon could include evaluating employee performance and recommending promotions, or disciplining or even firing a subordinate.

Entertaining is a big part of a Foreign Service officer's life—either having local people or people from other embassies to dinner or going to dinner at someone else's house. There, they learn a lot about what's going on in the country from talking to other diplomats and the people who live there. On weekends, officers can travel around the country and see the sights in other cities—not only just to play tourist but to meet other people and talk to them. "What I like most about being an administrative officer in the Foreign Service is the opportunity to see a problem, determine what the solution is," Van Laningham says, "and then see it through to the end. Obviously, travel is also a very attractive part of the job. You can live overseas in a country for a number of years and really get to know what it's like in depth."

He was posted in Iraq when Saddam Hussein invaded Kuwait and had been scheduled to fly home to attend his high school reunion, but, of course, there were no planes leaving the country. The Foreign Service evacuated most of the staff from the American embassy in Baghdad but had about one hundred people from the Kuwait embassy who were trying to get back to the United States. First, they received permission to leave, but then things changed. Van Laningham spent three days trying to secure exit visas.

The permission finally came through at about three o'clock in the morning, Iraq time, which, Van Laningham remembered, was exactly when his high school reunion had been scheduled in the States. "I knew the telephone number where the reunion was being held," he says, "so I called and ended up talking to about forty of my former classmates over the phone. Between that and having just succeeded in getting visas for a hundred people to get out of the country, it made a wonderful experience, one that I won't quickly forget."

Frustrations include working within the State Department, a giant organization with occasionally competing interests and the difficulty of getting multiple levels of approval for a specific course of action. And tight budgets mean less money to carry out the work.

But Van Laningham calls it a fabulous career. Every day is different. The travel possibilities are the envy of many an American bound to a stateside job. And with twenty years of service, Foreign Service employees can retire at age fifty. "For me, there's a lot of excitement about being able to represent the United States overseas," he says, "meeting important people in the country where you are living and perhaps even affecting how relations develop between the United States and that country."

Advice from Jim Van Laningham.   Van Laningham doesn't see one particular field of study leading to the Foreign Service. He says the people he knows have taken many different routes to the field. The common thread is that they were well-rounded, multitalented, and highly educated. Foreign Service officers have to be able to write well and organize thoughts logically and coherently. They also must be outgoing because they deal with a lot of different people on a daily basis. This is a diplomat's job, and tact, political savvy, and brinksmanship are all part of the toolkit.

Van Laningham cites an interest in the world around you as crucial, as one of an officer's primary responsibilities is to report back to Washington on what's happening in the country he's in. "You have to have leadership ability," he says. "It also helps to be familiar with finances and budgets."

Resources

Canada
Foreign Affairs Canada
Information on traveling and living abroad, international affairs
fac-aec.gc.ca/menu-en.asp

Jobs.gc.ca
Canadian government's central site for federal government jobs
jobs-emplois.gc.ca

Rates of Pay for the Public Service of Canada
Categorized by occupation
tbs-sct.gc.ca/pubs_pol/hrpubs/RatesofPay/Ra97_e.asp

United States
Careers in the Foreign Service
Responsibilities, career paths, how to apply
careers.state.gov/opportunities/index.html

Department of State
Information on traveling and living abroad, international affairs
state.gov

Federal Pay Schedules
Click on "Salaries and Wages," then "General Schedule and Locality
    Pay Tables"
opm.gov/flsa/oca/

FedWorld
A jumping-off point for access to government websites
fedworld.gov

Government Internships
Current listing of available government internships
usajobs.opm.gov/EI-13.asp
The Job Page
Listings for state and local government jobs
thejobpage.gov/statelocal.asp

Student Jobs
Temporary and long-term employment for students
studentjobs.gov

USAJobs
Comprehensive resource for federal government jobs
usajobs.opm.gov

Path 2: Marketing

Companies that are hiring for marketing positions interview applicants with all kinds of backgrounds. Business degrees are common, certainly, but so are liberal arts degrees. Many job postings simply ask for a bachelor's degree and let interviewers make decisions based on candidates rather than resumes. Yet economics majors, with their B-school savvy and broad academic palette, have an advantage and are increasingly in demand. For more technical positions, hiring managers like the fact that economics majors feel comfortable with numbers after having taken courses in accounting, finance, statistics, and mathematics; economics majors also possess the "big-picture" perspective that comes from exposure to business law, social sciences, government, and history. Several areas of marketing should interest economics majors. Here we'll discuss marketing research analysts, marketing managers, sales managers, and public relations managers.

Marketing Research Analysts

Marketing research analysts are concerned with the potential sales of a product or service. They analyze statistical data on past sales to predict future sales. They gather data on competitors and analyze prices, sales, and methods of marketing and distribution.

Marketing research analysts engage in research to find out how well products or services are received by the market. This may include the planning, implementation, and analysis of surveys to determine people's needs and preferences.

Similar to economists, marketing research analysts devise methods and procedures for obtaining the data they need. They often design online, telephone, mail, or in-person interview surveys to assess consumer preferences. Telephone and in-person surveys are usually conducted by trained interviewers under the marketing research analyst's direction. Once the data are compiled, marketing research analysts evaluate it. They then make recommendations to their client or employer based on their findings. They provide a company's management with information needed to make decisions on the promotion, distribution, design, and pricing of company products or services, or to determine the advisability of adding new lines of merchandise, opening new branches, or otherwise diversifying the company's operations.

Analysts also may conduct opinion research to determine the public's attitudes on various issues. This can help political or business leaders assess support for their electoral prospects or advertising policies.

Market research firms use econometric and statistical techniques to forecast the demand for alternative products. These firms conduct and analyze survey data to estimate the potential market for new or revised products. Some of the higher-quality market research firms use sophisticated econometric techniques to estimate the own-price, cross-price, and income elasticities of demands for alternative products. They also use census data to examine the demographic structure of alternative geographical markets.

Marketing Managers

The executive vice president for marketing in large firms directs the overall marketing policy, including market research, marketing strategy, sales, advertising, promotion, pricing, product development, and public relations activities. These activities are supervised by middle and supervisory managers who oversee staffs of professionals and technicians.

Marketing managers develop the firm's detailed marketing strategy. With the help of staff, including product development managers and market research managers, they determine the demand for products and services offered by the firm and its competitors and identify potential consumers, such as business firms, wholesalers, retailers, governments, or the general public. They further categorize mass markets according to various factors such as region, age, income, and lifestyle.

Marketing managers develop pricing strategy with an eye toward maximizing the firm's share of the market and its profits while ensuring that the firm's customers are satisfied. In collaboration with sales managers, product development managers, and other managers, they monitor trends that indicate the need for new products and services and oversee product development.

Marketing managers work with advertising and promotion managers to best promote the firm's products and services and to attract potential users.

Sales Managers

Sales managers direct the firms' sales programs. They assign sales territories, set goals, and establish training programs for their sales representatives. Managers advise their sales representatives on ways to improve sales performance. In large, multiproduct firms, they oversee local and regional sales managers and their staffs. Sales managers maintain contact with dealers and distributors. They analyze sales statistics gathered by their staffs to determine sales potential and inventory requirements and monitor the preferences of customers. Such information is vital to developing products and maximizing profits.

Public Relations Managers

Public relations managers direct publicity programs to a targeted public. They use any necessary communications media in their efforts to maintain the support of the specific group upon whom their organizations' success depends, such as consumers, stockholders, or the general public. For example, public relations managers may clarify or justify the firm's point of view on health or environmental issues to community or special-interest groups. They may evaluate advertising and promotion programs for compatibility with public relations efforts.

Public relations managers, in effect, serve as the eyes and ears of top management. They observe social, economic, and political trends that might ultimately have an effect upon the firm, and they make recommendations to enhance the firm's public image in view of those trends. Public relations managers may confer with labor-relations managers to produce internal company communications, such as news about employee-management relations, and consult with financial managers to produce company reports. They may assist company executives in drafting speeches, arranging interviews, and other forms of public contact. They might also oversee company archives and respond to information requests. In addition, public relations managers may handle special events, such as sponsorship of races, planning parties to introduce new products, and other activities the firm supports in order to gain public attention through the press without advertising directly.

Possible Job Settings

Market research analysts, marketing managers, sales managers, and public relations managers find employment in a variety of settings, including government agencies, manufacturers, economic consulting firms, financial institutions, research and development consulting firms, market research firms, motor vehicle dealers, printing and publishing firms, advertising agencies, department stores, computer and data-processing services firms, and management and public relations firms.

Working Conditions

Working conditions in marketing can be tough but are not uniform between various positions.

Market Research Analysts

Like economists, marketing research analysts have structured work schedules, often working alone writing reports and preparing statistical charts. But some job settings require the marketing research analyst to work as a part of a research team. The work involves pressure of deadlines, tight schedules, and often overtime.

Marketing, Sales, and Public Relations Managers

Marketing, sales, and public relations managers are provided with offices close to top managers. Long hours, including evenings and weekends, are common. Working under pressure is unavoidable as schedules change, problems arise, and deadlines and goals must be met.

Marketing, advertising, and public relations managers meet frequently with other managers; some meet with the public and with government officials. Substantial travel may be involved. For example, attendance at meetings sponsored by associations or industries is often mandatory. Sales managers travel to national, regional, and local offices and to various dealers and distributors. Advertising and promotion managers may travel to meet with clients or media representatives. Public relations managers may travel to meet with special-interest groups or government officials. Job transfers between headquarters and regional offices are common, particularly among sales managers, and may disrupt family life.

Preparing for the Work

Many economics students don't immediately think of marketing as a career path, but more marketers are relying on them. You can enter the field with a bachelor's or an advance degree, but the wise student will accrue some experience in the field before seeking a full-time job.

Marketing Research Analyst

Whether working in government, industry, research organizations, marketing, or consulting firms, economists and marketing research analysts who have graduate degrees usually qualify for more responsible research and administrative positions. A Ph.D. is necessary for top economist or marketing positions in many organizations. Many corporate and government executives have strong backgrounds in economics or marketing.

Graduate training is required for most private-sector marketing research analyst jobs and for advancement to more responsible positions. Market research analysts may earn advanced degrees in economics, business administration, marketing, statistics, or some closely related discipline.

Even before you graduate, getting on-the-job experience in the form of internships, co-ops, or work-study programs will make you more attractive to companies that are hiring and demonstrate your seriousness about entering the field. Some schools help graduate students find internships or part-time employment in government agencies, economic consulting firms, financial institutions, or marketing research firms prior to graduation. This early experience can also help you decide whether a marketing job is right for you.

A bachelor's degree with a major in economics or marketing is generally not sufficient to obtain a position as a marketing analyst, but it is excellent preparation for many entry-level positions, including research assistant, administrative or management trainee, marketing interviewer, or numerous professional sales jobs.

Aspiring market research analysts should gain experience gathering and analyzing data, conducting interviews and surveys, and writing reports on their findings while in college. This experience can prove invaluable later in obtaining a full-time position in the field, since much of the work, in the beginning, may revolve around these duties. Experience with database, spreadsheet, and statistical software is also important.

In addition, employers look for well-developed interpersonal and language skills. Market research analysts must be able to present their findings, both verbally and in writing, in a clear, meaningful way. Good communication, an ability to work with many different types of personalities, and a grounding in conflict resolution are valuable.

With experience, market research analysts eventually are assigned their own research projects. Those considering careers as market research analysts should be able to work accurately, because much time is spent on data analysis. Patience and persistence are necessary, since market research analysts must spend long hours on independent study and problem solving. At the same time, they must work well with others; market research analysts often oversee interviews for a wide variety of individuals.

Marketing, Sales, and Public Relations Managers

A wide range of educational backgrounds are suitable for entry into marketing, sales, and public relations managerial jobs, but many employers prefer a broad liberal arts background. A bachelor's degree in economics, sociology, psychology, literature, or philosophy, among other subjects, is acceptable. However, requirements vary depending upon the particular job.

For marketing and sales management positions, some employers prefer a bachelor's or master's degree in business administration with an emphasis on marketing. Courses in economics, business law, accounting, finance, mathematics, and statistics are also highly recommended. In highly technical industries, such as computer and electronics manufacturing, a bachelor's degree in engineering or science combined with a master's degree in business administration may be preferable.

For public relations management positions, some employers prefer a bachelor's or master's degree in public relations or journalism. The individual's curriculum should include courses in advertising, business administration, public affairs, political science, and creative and technical writing. For all these specialties, courses in management and completion of an internship while in school are highly recommended. Familiarity with computerized word processing and database applications also are important for many marketing and public relations management positions.

Most of these management positions are filled by promoting experienced staff or related professional or technical personnel, such as sales representatives, purchasing agents, buyers, product or brand specialists, advertising specialists, promotion specialists, and public relations specialists.

In small firms, where the number of positions is limited, advancement to a management position may come slowly. In large firms, you may get promoted more quickly.

Although experience, ability, and leadership are emphasized for promotion, advancement may be accelerated by participation in the management-training programs that many large firms conduct. Many firms also provide their employees with continuing-education opportunities, either in-house or at local colleges and universities, and encourage employee participation in seminars and conferences, often held by professional societies. In collaboration with colleges and universities, numerous marketing and related associations sponsor national or local management training programs. Courses include brand and product management, international marketing, sales management evaluation, telemarketing and direct sales, promotion, marketing communication, market research, organizational communication, and data-processing systems procedures and management. Many firms pay all or part of the cost for those who successfully complete courses.

Some associations, a number of which are listed in Appendix A, offer certification programs for marketing, advertising, and public relations managers. Certification is a sign of competence and achievement that is particularly important in a competitive job market. While relatively few marketing, sales, and public relations managers currently are certified, the number of managers seeking certification is expected to grow. For example, Sales and Marketing Executives International (smei.org) offers a management certification program based on education and job performance. The Public Relations Society of America (prsa.org) offers an accreditation program for public relations practitioners based on years of experience and an examination. The American Marketing Association (ama.org) offers a Professional Certified Marketer (PCM) program to recognize marketing professionals' expertise.

People interested in becoming marketing, sales, and public relations managers should be mature, creative, highly motivated, resistant to stress, and flexible yet decisive. The ability to communicate persuasively, both verbally and in writing, with other managers, staff, and the public is vital.

Marketing, sales, and public relations managers also need tact, good judgment, and an exceptional ability to establish and maintain effective personal relationships with supervisory and professional staff members and client firms.

Because of the importance and high visibility of their jobs, marketing, sales, and public relations managers often are prime candidates for advancement. Well-trained, experienced, successful managers may be promoted to higher positions in their own or other firms. Some become top executives. Managers with extensive experience and sufficient capital may open their own businesses.

Career Outlook

Job prospects in marketing are competitive but promising.

Marketing Research Analysts

Employment of marketing research analysts is expected to grow faster than the average for all occupations through 2014. Many job openings are likely to result from the need to replace experienced workers who transfer to other occupations, retire, or leave the labor force for other reasons.

Demand for qualified marketing research analysts should be strong due to an increasingly competitive economy. Marketing research provides organizations with valuable feedback from purchasers, allowing companies to evaluate consumer satisfaction and more effectively plan for the future.

With companies seeking to expand their market and as consumers become better informed, the need for marketing professionals is increasing. Opportunities for market research analysts with graduate degrees should be good in a wide range of employment settings, particularly in marketing research irms, as companies find it more profitable to contract out for marketing research services rather than support their own marketing department.

Other organizations, including financial services organizations, health care institutions, advertising agencies, manufacturing firms producing consumer goods, and insurance companies, may offer job opportunities for market research analysts.

A strong background in marketing, mathematics, statistics, and econometrics provides the basis for developing any specialty within the field. Similar to economists, marketing research graduates with related work experience in a closely related business field or industry should have the best job opportunities.

Those with only bachelor's degrees but who have strong backgrounds in mathematics, statistics, survey design, and computer science may be hired by private firms as research assistants.

Marketing, Sales, and Public Relations Managers

These jobs are highly coveted and will be sought by other managers or highly experienced professional and technical personnel, resulting in substantial job competition. College graduates with extensive experience, a high level of creativity, and strong communication skills should have the best job opportunities. Those who have interactive (Internet-based) marketing skills will be particularly sought after.

Employment of marketing, sales, and public relations managers is expected to increase faster than the average for all occupations through 2014. Increasingly intense domestic and global competition in products and services offered to consumers should require greater marketing, promotional, and public relations efforts by managers. Management and public relations firms may experience particularly rapid growth as businesses increasingly hire contractors for these services rather than support additional full-time staff.

Projected employment growth varies by industry. For example, employment of marketing, sales, and public relations managers is expected to grow faster than average in most business-services industries, such as computer and data-processing and management and public relations firms, while forecasters project an overall decline in manufacturing.

Salaries

According to a recent salary survey by the National Association of Colleges and Employers, graduates with bachelor's degrees in marketing received offers averaging $36,409, and those with bachelor's degrees in economics received notably higher offers, averaging $41,994 a year.

The median annual salary for marketing managers in 2004 was $87,640. For sales managers, it was somewhat lower: $84,220. The median for public relations managers was $70,000. The salary scale in marketing is broad compared with most industries. In addition to the typical variables of region, company size, and work experience, pay for sales and marketing managers varies based on the company's specific industry and the position's responsibilities, which can vary drastically from job to job. Manufacturing firms pay managers higher salaries than nonmanufacturing firms do, for example. Marketing managers working in computer systems and related services earn much higher median salaries ($107,030 in 2004) than the industry average, as do those in business management ($98,700 in 2004). For sales managers, pay varies according to the industry, the size of the sales region covered, and, of course, performance. Many earn bonuses equal to 10 percent or more of their salaries. See the table below for a sampling of salaries for related positions, with job descriptions.

MEDIAN U.S. SALARIES FOR TOP MARKETING POSITIONS

Position	Salary	Total Comp.
Vice president, advertising: Counsels and coordinates all organization divisions. Aids marketing personnel in all divisions in developing marketing plans, creating ad themes, and selecting media. Typically reports to the top sales and marketing officer.	$106,073	$137,073
Vice president, public relations: Leads, manages and directs organization's public relations efforts. Typically reports to chief executive officer or chief operations officer.	$109,000	$141,980
Advertising supervisor: Supervises the operations of an advertising department with administration of sales policies and programs. Typically reports to advertising manager and is the first level of supervision.	$60,548	$72,192
Account executive: Promotes, plans, develops, coordinates, and directs advertising campaign for clients, liaising with both clients and in-house staff.	46,574	56,034

Source: Baker, Thomsen Associates Insurance Services, Inc., SalaryExpert.com.

Sample Job Ads

The job ads below reflect a range of educational and experience levels and can offer a sense of the skills current employers want.

Job Title: Marketing Coordinator
Experience: Bachelor's degree, one to two years in marketing or related field
Location: Ft. Lauderdale, Florida

Description: High-energy individual with strong analytical and creative skills needed to help drive sales of the company's line of training and test-preparation products. Primary responsibility is to identify and implement advertising campaigns and lead-generation initiatives that promote marketing efficiency and distribution. Coordinator will

- Develop sales support collateral
- Assist in developing and optimizing phone sales scripts
- Provide direct marketing support for sales initiatives
- Assist with market research and competitor analysis
- Monitor and maintain a strong Internet presence through search engine optimization practices

Requirements

- Ability to handle a variety of tasks in a deadline-oriented environment
- Strong analytical skills and follow-through
- Strong communication and interpersonal skills
- Ability to manage multiple projects at the same time

Previous lead-generation experience preferred. Salary $27,000 to $38,000 depending on qualifications and experience. Benefits include medical, dental, vision, and 401(k).

Job Title: Marketing Manager/Analyst
Experience: Bachelor's degree, two to five years in marketing or related field
Location: New York City

Description: The world's leading international insurance and financial services organization seeks a marketing manager/analyst to perform a wide variety of marketing support services and communication to the Voluntary Employee Benefits organization. Duties will entail

- Assisting in the standardization of projects, such as collecting best marketing practices, conducting business plan analysis, and standardizing business processes and benchmarks
- Contributing to presentations and writing quarterly newsletters, presentations
- Promoting education and communication between the home office and twenty-five satellite offices around the world

Requirements

- Strong verbal and written communication skills and the ability to interact with all levels of management
- Excellent organizational skills and attention to detail
- Proficiency in MS Word, Excel, and PowerPoint
- Previous marketing support experience or MBA preferred

Job Title: Vice President of Marketing and New Product Development
Experience: Bachelor's plus MBA, ten to fifteen years in the field
Location: Minneapolis, Minnesota

Description: The Vice President of Marketing and NPD will manage a group of ten and lead the development and implementation of product and business strategies for this company. Responsibilities will include

- Pursuing acquisitions as the primary growth vehicle
- Developing and executing business strategies and marketing plans in each of the business categories in which the company competes
- Managing the development and commercialization of new products
- Identifying and developing plans to expand existing markets and enter new geographic markets
- Strengthening the company's value proposition in all markets by focusing on sustainable competitive advantages in order to ensure that the company maintains its market leadership position
- Directing the company's marketing communications function, including trade shows, advertising, press relations, and promotional campaigns
- Directing and developing all sales and marketing collateral materials

Requirements:

- High level of business acumen, including P&L (profit-and-loss) management
- A demonstrated track record of achieving results through the development and execution of formal marketing plans and strategies

continued

- Demonstrated ability to manage and develop employees and the ability to interface with operations, finance, and the customer
- Personal qualities include honesty, maturity, ethical and professional behavior, and a high degree of integrity

VP will report to president/CEO. Experience in consumer packaged goods as well as commercial products desirable. Sales experience is a plus. Experience in new product development, including a successful track record in launching new product introductions, preferred. Total compensation up to $250,000. Position holder in line to succeed president/CEO.

Close-Up

Chris Fuller, General Manager, Marketing and Sales

Chris Fuller worked in marketing and sales for more than thirty years, from middle management to the executive corridor. Although he's now retired, Fuller worked for such Fortune 500 companies and related brands as Colgate-Palmolive; General Foods, a part of Kraft Foods; Pepsi Cola; and Lipton, part of Unilever. He earned both his BA (in economics) and his MBA from Dartmouth College. Much of his experience was in food service. Even his first job out of school with Colgate-Palmolive, which is in the household products business, involved selling through the same channels as the food companies, and the products ended up in the same stores. "It was glamorous in a way," Fuller says of his attraction to marketing. "You had a lot of advertising and promotion. Product managers made good money, the businesses were stable, and you didn't have the big hiring and firing problems" that you see today.

At General Foods, Fuller was a manager of marketing analysis and then became a product manager in the frozen potato business. Later, at Pepsi Cola, he was vice president of finance and president of Metrop Bottling Company, which sold Pepsi through company-owned franchises in the United States. He ended his career with Lipton, where he was senior vice president of operations and finance before becoming senior vice president of general management. Even at the top at Lipton, he essentially held a marketing job, managing a group of businesses.

On the Job. Retail food operations deal with chain supermarkets and mom-and-pop stores. The purpose of the food-service industry, by contrast, is to sell products to restaurants and cafeterias and increase their exposure. It's a small subset of the retail business for such giants as Kraft, Nabisco, and Procter & Gamble and is usually less profitable. At Lipton, Fuller oversaw a number of product lines, from Good Humor ice cream to Sahadi, a Middle

Eastern-oriented line that included fruit rolls and other products. Lipton also has a dry-soup business, Wishbone salad dressing, and noodles-and-sauce and rice-and-sauce businesses.

One function of food service is to take the retail products and redesign them in the appropriate packaging for restaurants. Often large-scale food-service operations require much larger volume, and products aren't competing on the shelves to catch a customer's eye. Fuller's work at Lipton is one example: A tea bag sold to a consumer is for one cup of tea. The tea bag sold to a restaurant might be for a whole jug of tea. The taste could be different as well. A company might sell a very spicy product, but the restaurant doesn't want a spicy product; it caters to milder tastes. "Sometimes you can accommodate them, sometimes you can't, depending on how many other restaurants are in the same boat," Fuller says.

Another function of food service is marketing: pricing, packaging, and the development of the particular product as it relates to advertising and promotion. Food-service divisions advertise in the trade journals to let customers know they're going to be offering a particular product. Marketing also includes sales. "We worked as part of a team," Fuller says. "We had a finance person, for example, who would tell us if we were making money or not or what kind of prices we needed in order to make a profit on something. This position often holds a profit responsibility. If he spends too much money, the business will lose money, and he's the guy who will go out the door."

Sales presented its own challenges because the salespeople tended to view transactions in terms of volume, quotas, and product support. They continually asked for lower prices and more advertising, whereas the marketing director had to mind the budget and ensure profitability as well as market penetration.

In one role, Fuller supervised the sales manager, who was in charge of day-to-day food service and would decide what pricing promotions and advertising were needed that month to sell the product. That person also decided how many salespeople he needed, what kind of training they should have, where they should be stationed, which accounts salespeople would call on, and how much time they would devote to each account. Because food service volume is generally lower than retail's volume, companies often can't take on too many salespeople. That means larger sales regions and tough travel schedules. "Sometimes the accounts will see you when you want to see them; sometimes you have to wait and see them another day and here you are, having traveled three hundred miles," Fuller says. "So, what are you going to do if you don't have it planned to see other accounts in that area?"

The sales manager also has to hit the road to meet with sales reps because they can't afford to lose sales by spending time in the office. So, the sales manager is out in the field with personnel too, making calls and ensuring the reps are using the right techniques and handling each situation the way it should be.

Once someone moves into marketing, the travel required decreases substantially. The sales manager normally reports to the vice president of marketing. However, marketing managers are responsible for profit and sales goals just as much as the sales reps are. Sales managers set benchmarks in concert with marketing, so if volume for a particular account doesn't meet expectations, marketing also has to pay the piper—perhaps more so since those employees are higher up on the food chain.

As you might expect, people drive the business. If an institution isn't growing and doesn't require higher food orders, a salesperson needs to build relationships to the point that the purchasing agent feels comfortable giving the supplier more business. As Fuller puts it, "You'd better get to know who their spouses and kids are, remember birthdays, and take them out to dinner. If you don't like walking in and talking to people every day, this job isn't for you," he says.

Just as with the rapport between salesperson and purchaser, much of the product value comes from reputation and brand recognition. Buyers don't have time to sample every food, and the sales rep's cooking skills might leave something to be desired anyway, so to a degree, buyers need to have accept the food on faith, and previous experience.

Money in food service is roughly equal to that in the retail food industry, Fuller says. Employees on both sides work in a competitive environment, and in sales, they can expect to see a fair number of incentives: trips, prizes, and cash.

Advice from Chris Fuller. The most important thing is that you don't mind traveling and that you like to meet people and talk to people every day. Beyond that, learn to take direction well. The industry is firmly structured and operates with regional managers or division managers providing explicit instructions on policies and goals. Sales is especially goal-oriented. Fuller calls it the fishbowl: "Every salesperson in the country has his working life on a computer somewhere."

Salespeople are the frontline image of the company. They serve as ambassadors, entertainers, and troubleshooters all at once. As such, they can expect flack from customers who think they were shorted or question the integrity of a certain shipment, and who probably just received a lecture from their superior. But when customers are happy, sales reps are the first ones to hear that, too. Fuller suggests trying to shift to the retail side after gaining some experience in food-service sales and then moving into marketing once you're in your early thirties. Remain in sales much past that time, he says, and you'll stay in sales. Transitioning to marketing has the added benefit of getting workers off the road about the same time they're starting families.

All in all, sales and marketing can offer rewarding, and in this case stable, careers for those who seek a new adventure behind every door.

Path 3: Human Resources

Economics majors choosing careers in human resource management are responsible for filling positions within a company, using an effective salary structure, designing and administering attractive benefits packages, and establishing the process and criteria for hiring and promotion.

Attracting high-value employees and matching them to the most appropriate jobs are important for the success of any organization. However, many enterprises are too large to permit close contact between top management and employees. Instead, personnel, training, and labor relations specialists and managers, commonly known as human resources specialists and managers, perform this duty. These individuals recruit and interview employees and advise on hiring decisions using policies and requirements established with direction from top management.

In an effort to improve morale and productivity and limit job turnover, they also help their firms effectively use employees' skills, provide training opportunities to enhance those skills, and boost employees' satisfaction with their jobs and working conditions.

Although some jobs in human resources require only limited contact with people outside the office, most involve frequent contact. Dealing with people is an essential part of the job. In a small organization, one person may handle all aspects of personnel, training, and labor relations work. In contrast, in a large corporation the top human resources executive usually develops and coordinates personnel programs and policies. Usually a director or manager of human resources (and, in some cases, a director of industrial relations) implements these policies.

Your Career Path

Within the human resources field, there's a wide range of job titles and responsibilities.

Human Resources Directors

The director of human resources may oversee several departments, each headed by an experienced manager, who most likely specializes in one personnel function, such as employment, compensation, benefits, training and development, or employee relations.

Employment Managers

Employment and placement managers oversee the hiring and separation of employees and supervise various workers, including equal employment opportunity specialists and recruitment specialists.

Recruiters

Recruiters maintain contacts within the community and may travel extensively—often to college campuses—to search for promising job applicants. Recruiters screen, interview, and, in some cases, test applicants. They may also check references and extend offers of employment to qualified candidates. These workers need to be thoroughly familiar with the organization and its personnel policies to discuss wages, working conditions, and promotional opportunities with prospective employees. They also need to keep informed about equal employment opportunity (EEO) and affirmative action guidelines and laws, such as the Americans with Disabilities Act (ADA).

EEO/Affirmative Action Coordinators

Large organizations often employ special EEO representatives or affirmative action coordinators. They investigate and resolve EEO grievances, examine corporate practices for possible violations, and compile and submit EEO statistical reports.

Employer Relations Representatives

Employer relations representatives, usually found in government agencies, maintain working relationships with local employers and promote the use of public employment programs and services.

Employment Interviewers

Employment interviewers, sometimes called personnel consultants, help match job seekers with employers.

Job Analysts

Job analysts, sometimes called position classifiers, perform very exacting work. They collect and examine detailed information about job duties to prepare job descriptions. These descriptions explain the duties, training, and skills each job requires. Whenever a large organization introduces a new job or reviews existing jobs, it calls upon the expert knowledge of the job analyst.

Occupational Analysts

Occupational analysts conduct research, generally in large firms. They are concerned with occupational classification systems and study the effects of industry and occupational trends upon worker relationships. They may serve as a technical liaison between the firm and industry, government, and labor unions.

Compensation Managers

Establishing and maintaining a firm's pay system is the principal job of the compensation manager. Assisted by staff specialists, compensation managers devise ways to ensure fair and equitable pay rates. They may conduct surveys to see how their rates compare with others and to ensure that the firm's pay scale complies with changing laws and regulations.

In addition, compensation managers often oversee their firm's performance evaluation system, and they may design reward systems such as pay-for-performance plans.

Employee Benefits Managers

Employee benefits managers handle the company's employee benefits program, notably its health insurance and 401(k) plans. Expertise in designing and administering benefits programs continues to gain importance as employer-provided benefits account for a growing proportion of overall compensation costs, and as benefit plans increase in number and complexity. For example, health benefits may include long-term disability, dental insurance, flexible spending accounts (a pretax account you contribute to and can later apply to uncovered medical expenses), and dependent care accounts, which are similar to flexible spending accounts but apply to daycare expenses. A company might match a percentage of the employee's 401(k) contributions and offer some kind of profit-sharing plan. Familiarity with health benefits is a top priority as companies are looking to lessen healthcare expenses and transfer more costs to employees.

In addition to health insurance and retirement accounts, some firms offer their employees life and accidental death and dismemberment insurance, disability insurance, and relatively new benefits designed to meet the needs of a changing workforce, such as flex time, parental leave, child care and elder care, long-term nursing home care insurance, employee assistance and wellness programs, and flexible benefits plans. Benefits managers must keep abreast of changing federal and state regulations and legislation that may affect employee benefits.

Employee Assistance Plan Managers

Employee assistance plan managers, also called employee welfare managers, are responsible for a wide array of programs covering occupational safety and health standards and practices; health promotion and physical fitness, medical examinations and minor health treatment, such as first aid; plant security; publications; food service and recreation activities; car pooling; employee suggestion systems; child care and elder care; and counseling services. Child and elder care are increasingly important with most parents working and as more Boomers reach retirement age. Counseling may help employees deal with emotional disorders, alcoholism, or marital, family, consumer, legal, and financial problems. In large firms, some of these programs, such as security and safety, are in separate departments headed by other managers.

Training and Development Managers

Training and development managers supervise training operations. Increasingly, management recognizes that training offers a way of developing skills, enhancing productivity and quality of work, and building loyalty to the firm. Training is widely accepted as a method of improving employee morale, but this is only one reason for its growing importance. Other factors include the complexity of the work environment, the rapid pace of organizational and technological change, and the growing number of jobs in fields that constantly generate new knowledge. In addition, advances in learning theory have provided insights into how adults learn and how training can be organized most effectively for them.

Training specialists plan, organize, and direct a wide range of training activities. Trainers conduct orientation sessions and arrange on-the-job training for new employees. They help rank-and-file workers maintain and improve their job skills and possibly prepare for jobs requiring greater skill. They help supervisors improve their interpersonal skills in order to deal effectively with employees. And they may set up individualized training plans to strengthen an employee's existing skills or to teach new ones.

Training specialists in some companies set up programs to develop executive potential among employees in lower-level positions.

In government-supported training programs, training specialists function as case managers. They first assess the training needs of clients, and then guide them through the most appropriate training methods. After training, clients may either be referred to employer relations representatives or receive job placement assistance.

Planning and program development is an important part of the training specialist's job. In order to identify and assess training needs within the firm, trainers may confer with managers and supervisors or conduct surveys. They also periodically evaluate training effectiveness.

Depending on the size, goals, and nature of the organization, trainers may differ considerably in their responsibilities and in the methods they use. Training methods include on-the-job training; schools in which shop conditions are duplicated for trainees prior to putting them on the shop floor; apprenticeship training; classroom training; programmed instruction, which may involve interactive videos, videodiscs, and other computer-aided instructional technologies; simulators; conferences; and workshops.

International Human Resources Managers

Less common but growing are the ranks of international human resources managers, who handle human resources issues related to a company's foreign operations. As companies save on labor by basing some work overseas, they also need HR managers to help train existing staff for work in a foreign country, assist foreign employees with the transition to working and living in North America, and coordinate company policies and procedures at international offices. Close familiarity with the cultures of those countries, and fluency in their languages, are great benefits.

Human Resources Information System Specialists

The human resources information system specialist is another emerging role. The specialist develops and applies computer programs to process personnel information, match job seekers with job openings, and handle other personnel matters.

Other Paths in Human Resources

Although often considered a separate field, labor and industrial relations can sometimes be part of the realm of human resources and is a viable career path for economics majors.

Industrial Relations Directors

The director of industrial relations forms labor policy, oversees industrial labor relations, negotiates collective bargaining agreements, and coordinates grievance procedures to handle complaints resulting from disputes under the contract for firms with unionized employees. The director of industrial relations also advises and collaborates with the director of human resources and other managers and members of their staff, because all aspects of personnel policy, such as wages, benefits, pensions, and work practices, may be involved in drawing up new or revised contracts.

Labor Relations Managers

Industrial labor relations programs are implemented by labor relations managers and their staffs. When a collective bargaining agreement is up for negotiation, labor relations specialists prepare information for management to use during negotiation, which requires familiarity with economic and wage data, as well as extensive knowledge of labor law and collective bargaining trends. The labor relations staff interprets and administers the contract with respect to grievances; wages and salaries; employee welfare; health care; pensions; union and management practices; and other contractual stipulations. As union membership continues to decline in most industries, industrial relations personnel are working more with nonunion employees.

Dispute Resolution Specialists

Dispute resolution—that is, attaining tacit or contractual agreements—has become increasingly important as parties to a dispute attempt to avoid costly litigation, strikes, or other disruptions. Dispute resolution also has become more complex, involving employees, management, unions, other firms, and government agencies. Specialists involved in dispute resolution must be highly knowledgeable and experienced, and they often report to the director of industrial relations.

A conciliator, or mediator, advises and counsels labor and management to prevent and, when necessary, resolve disputes over labor agreements or other labor relations issues.

An arbitrator, sometimes called an umpire or referee, decides disputes that bind both labor and management to specific terms and conditions of labor contracts.

Labor relations specialists who work for unions perform many of the same functions on behalf of the union and its members.

Preparing for the Work

Because of the diversity of duties and level of responsibility, the educational backgrounds of human resources, personnel, training, and labor relations specialists and managers vary considerably.

In filling entry-level jobs, firms generally seek college graduates. Some employers prefer applicants who have majored in economics, human resources, personnel administration, or industrial and labor relations, while others look for college graduates with a technical or business background. Still others feel that a well-rounded liberal arts graduate is best.

Because an interdisciplinary background is appropriate for work in this area, a combination of courses in the social sciences, business, and behavioral sciences is useful. Some jobs may require a background in engineering, science, finance, or law. Most prospective personnel specialists should take courses in compensation, recruitment, training and development, and performance appraisal, as well as courses in principles of management, organizational structure, and industrial psychology. Other relevant courses include business administration, public administration, psychology, sociology, political science, economics, and statistics.

Courses in labor law, collective bargaining, labor economics, labor history, and industrial psychology also provide a valuable background for the prospective labor relations specialist. Knowledge of computers and information systems is important for some jobs.

Graduate study in industrial or labor relations is increasingly important for those seeking work in labor relations. A law degree seldom is required for entry-level jobs, but many people responsible for contract negotiations are lawyers, and a combination of industrial relations courses and law is highly desirable. A background in law is also desirable for employee benefits managers and others who must interpret the growing number of laws and regulations.

A degree in dispute resolution provides an excellent background for mediators, arbitrators, and related personnel. A master's degree in personnel, training, labor relations, a subspecialty of economics, or in business administration with a concentration in human resources management is desirable for those seeking general and top management positions.

For many specialized jobs in this field, previous experience is an asset; for managerial positions, it is essential. Many employers prefer entry-level workers who have gained some experience through an internship or work-study program while in school. Personnel administration and human resources development require the ability to work with individuals, as well as a commitment to organizational goals. This field also demands other skills that can be developed elsewhere—computer literacy, spreadsheet and database familiarity, selling, teaching, supervising, and volunteering, among others.

Personnel, training, and labor relations specialists and managers should speak and write effectively and be able to work with and/or supervise people of all levels of education and experience as part of a team. They must be tolerant of conflicting points of view and emotionally stable to deal with the unexpected and the unusual. The ability to function under pressure is essential.

Integrity, fair-mindedness, and a persuasive, congenial personality are important qualities.

Recent economics graduates can start as entry-level workers, often participating in formal or on-the-job training programs in which they learn how to classify jobs, interview applicants, or administer employee benefits. Next, they are assigned to specific areas in the personnel department to gain experience. Later, they may advance to managerial positions, overseeing a major element of the personnel program—compensation or training, for example.

Exceptional personnel, training, and labor relations workers may be promoted to directors of personnel or industrial relations, which can eventually lead to top managerial or executive positions. Others may join consulting firms or open their own businesses.

Though not widespread, some organizations offer certification exams to members who meet certain requirements for education and experience. Certification is proof of competence and can enhance one's advancement opportunities. (Several of these organizations are listed in Appendix A.)

Job Settings

Personnel, training, and labor relations specialists and managers hold 820,000 jobs in the United States. They are employed in virtually every industry. Specialists account for four out of five positions; managers, one out of five. About 21,000—mostly specialists—are self-employed, working as consultants to public and private employers.

The private sector accounts for more than 80 percent of salaried U.S. jobs. Among these salaried jobs, 11 percent come from administrative and support services; 9 percent from professional, scientific, and technical services; 9 percent from manufacturing; 9 percent from health care and social assistance; and 9 percent from finance and insurance firms.

Career Outlook

The number of personnel, training, and labor relations specialists and managers is expected to grow faster than the average for all occupations through 2014. As in other occupations, job growth among specialists is projected to outpace job growth among managers. In addition, many job openings will result from the need to replace workers who leave this occupation to transfer to other jobs, retire, or leave for other reasons.

Legislation and court rulings setting standards in various areas—occupational safety and health, equal employment opportunity, wages, health care, pensions, and family leave, among others—will increase demand for human resources, training, and labor relations experts. Rising health care costs should continue to spur demand for specialists to develop creative compensation and benefits packages that firms can offer prospective employees. Employment of labor relations staff, including arbitrators and mediators, should grow as firms become more involved in labor relations, and attempt to resolve potentially costly labor-management disputes out of court. Additional job growth may stem from increasing demand for specialists in international human resources management and human resources information systems.

Demand may be particularly strong for certain specialists. For example, employers are expected to devote greater resources to job-specific training programs in response to the increasing complexity of many jobs, the aging of the workforce, and technological advances that can leave employees with obsolete skills. This should result in strong demand for training and development specialists. In addition, increasing efforts throughout industry to recruit and retain quality employees should create many jobs for employment, recruitment, and placement specialists.

Among industries, firms involved in management, consulting, and employment services should offer many job opportunities, as businesses increasingly contract out human resources functions or hire human resources specialists on a temporary basis in order to deal with the increasing cost and complexity of training and development programs. Demand also should increase in firms that develop and administer complex employee benefits and compensation packages for other organizations.

Demand for human resources, training, and labor relations managers and specialists also are governed by the staffing needs of the firms for which they work. A rapidly expanding business is likely to hire additional human resources workers—either as permanent employees or consultants—while a business that has experienced a merger or a reduction in its workforce will require fewer human resources workers. Also, as human resources management becomes increasingly important to the success of an organization, some small and medium size businesses that do not have human resources departments may assign employees various human resources duties together with other unrelated responsibilities. In any particular firm, the size and the job duties of the human resources staff are determined by the firm's organizational philosophy and goals, skills of its workforce, pace of technological change, government regulations, collective bargaining agreements, standards of professional practice, and labor market conditions.

Job growth could be limited by the widespread use of computerized human resources information systems that make workers more productive. Like that of other workers, employment of human resources, training, and labor relations managers and specialists, particularly in larger firms, may be adversely affected by corporate downsizing, restructuring, and mergers.

Salaries

According to a 2005 salary survey conducted by the National Association of Colleges and Employers, applicants with bachelor's degrees entering human resources fields, including labor relations, received starting offers averaging $36,967.

In 2004, the median annual salaries for these HR-related positions were as follows:

Compensation and benefits managers	$66,530
Training and development managers	$67,460
All other human resources managers	$81,810
Employment, recruitment, and placement specialists	$41,190

Among those industries employing the largest numbers of employment, recruitment, and placement specialists, earnings were:

Management, scientific, and technical consulting services	$52,800
Management of companies and enterprises	$46,780
Local government	$40,540
Employment services	$37,780
State government	$35,390

Median annual salaries in 2004 for compensation, benefits, and job analysis specialists were $47,490. Median annual earnings in the industries employing the largest numbers of compensation, benefits, and job analysis specialists were:

Local government	$51,430
Management of companies and enterprises	$50,970
State government	$39,150

Median annual salaries in 2004 for training and development specialists were $44,570. Median annual earnings in the industries employing the largest numbers of training and development specialists were:

Management of companies and enterprises	$49,540
Insurance carriers	$47,300
Local government	$45,320
State government	$41,770
Federal government	$38,930

Employee relations specialists in the federal government averaged $84,847 in 2005; human resources managers averaged $71,232. The average labor relations specialist earned $93,895; and the average employee development specialist earned $80,958.

Sample Job Ads

To get an idea of the kind of positions available, examine the sample job announcements in Exhibits 8.1 through 8.6.

Close-Up

Robyn Bramhall, Senior Recruiter

Robyn Bramhall works in the human resources department at Fair, Isaac & Company in San Rafael, California. Previously, she had been in the sales department of a large bank and wanted work that brought her closer to people. A friend suggested technical recruiting since she had spent five years placing computer professionals on contract assignments. Another recruiter tipped her off about the opening at Fair, Isaac & Company, and Bramhall thought it seemed ideal—closer to home but still in a corporate environment, as opposed to an agency. "I still get to sell," she says, "but now it is selling a job and a company to a candidate—and then selling the candidate to the manager."

On the Job. Bramhall locates, qualifies, and presents candidates for certain types of positions. The work entails lots of phone calls, e-mails, record keeping, database searches, networking, advertising, and meetings. Some days it's lots of paperwork, as when she has just filled a position or needs to start a

Exhibit 8.1
CONSULTANT ANNOUNCEMENT

Job Title: Senior Manager, Human Capital Consulting
Location: New York City

Description: We have an opportunity for a senior manager with strong consulting and financial services industry experience to join our dynamic, innovative team. Team works with senior HR leaders and overall company executives to develop strategic HR solutions for today's workforce challenges and triple bottom-line impact. Our solutions include

- People strategy: The design and implementation of strategies, programs, and processes necessary to build the human capital required to execute business strategies.
- HR transformation: Realignment of the HR function (people, process, organization, and technology) to better support organizational goals.
- Workforce transitions: Helping companies manage the movement of resources as a result of a significant organizational event—e.g., merger, consolidation, and divestiture.
- HR: The optimization of resources through time and attendance, scheduling and modeling software solutions, as well as point solutions for human resources technology.

Responsibilities: Responsible for initiating and sustaining the development of client relationships primarily within the financial services industry and participating in building strong project teams in support of the Human Capital Optimization Solutions Group. Sales and delivery responsibility may include

- Design and implementation of workforce development strategies such as competency development, skill assessments, recruiting strategies, and employee satisfaction surveys.
- Design and implementation of world-class HR functions, including service delivery model alignment, Business Process Reengineering (BPR), ROI development, and outsourcing analysis.
- Design, coaching, and program management associated with redeploying, reducing, and/or retaining workforce resources as a result of organizational initiatives specifically to build processes for identifying, selecting, and exiting of workforce with a large-scale employee displacement.

Requirements: Must have 10+ years of HR experience, excellent knowledge and experience in management consulting and project management, prior experience in financial services, a strong network of relationships, and the ability to build a strong client base. The ideal candidate will have had experience with human capital issues on a global scale. Candidates must also be willing to travel extensively (more than 50 percent). Master's degree required.

Exhibit 8.2
HUMAN RESOURCES MANAGER ANNOUNCEMENT

Job Title: International Staffing Manager
Location: Redmond, Washington

Description: We have a unique opportunity for a well-seasoned staffing professional who is an expert at leading teams and building and executing staffing strategies, and who has a passion for recruiting . This person will be a key member of the HR team and will be responsible for leading the international staffing agenda. If you have global staffing experience and are an excellent leader known for your ability to build strong business partnerships and strong teams, recruit great talent, and continue to move the business forward, then this is the opportunity for you.

Responsibilities: Key accountabilities include building creative staffing solutions and alternatives; aligning staffing resources against critical business needs; evangelizing our staffing strategy to embrace quality, quantity, and diversity; effectively leveraging internal resources, tools, and systems to ensure maximum productivity and efficiency; building and motivating teams; and building strong business knowledge and strong partnerships with the HR generalist team to provide support to the business.

Requirements: 8–10 years of staffing experience including at least 3–4 years in a management role is preferred. Position location is flexible. Company offers an excellent benefits package to full-time employees including medical, dental, vacation, employee stock-purchase plan, and 401(k), plus extras, such as product discounts and paid infant-care leave.

Exhibit 8.3
LABOR RELATIONS ANNOUNCEMENT

Job Title: Labor Relations Specialist
Location: Columbus, Indiana

Description: Regardless of your degree or area of expertise, you'll have the capacity and the opportunity to immediately impact our organization and our future. We give you the freedom to take charge, the opportunities to grow, and the benefits to build your future. Our commitment to a solid work/life balance is just one example. We're looking for a detail-oriented team player with good development and problem-solving skills and a strong commitment to customer satisfaction to handle day-to-day administration of the office clerical unit (OCU) and dislocated workers unit (DWU) Labor Agreements across southern Indiana, as well as provide support for collective bargaining processes. This work includes problem solving, grievance management, arbitration preparations, contract interpretation, project management, conflict management, investigations, and PC skills.

Responsibilities: Successful candidate will manage a supervisor development training program, process development and implementation, quality improvements, and line HR support. This work also strongly supports the OCU and DWU Team Based Work System continuous development. Employee must be able to work independently of others, be self-motivated to complete individual and team goals, demonstrate proven process-improvement and project-management skills, and possess above-average computer skills (Excel, Access, etc.).

Requirements: The qualified candidate must have 3–5 years in the area of labor relations or 5+ years' experience in an operations role with heavy labor relations exposure. BS degree in related field, such as employee-labor relations or economics, preferred. Small amount of travel required. Company offers progressive benefits such as stock options and coverage for domestic partners as well as 401(k) and a full complement of personal and professional benefits. EOE.

---

visa process. Other days she spends at job fairs talking to dozens of people about the company's work.

Bramhall says the variety of work, interaction, and settings keeps her engaged and fresh. Yet there's always more to do. "Knowing that there's always something else I could be doing to get good people hired, I have to accept

Exhibit 8.4
CONTRACTS ADMINISTRATION ANNOUNCEMENT

Job Title: Contracts administrator
Location: Toronto, Ontario

Description: Responsible for the management of the contract life cycle from inception to completion, which includes development, negotiation, administration, and management of complex and high-risk contracts, includes long-term product support to ensure subcontractor support of business objectives and customer prime contract flow-down requirements on supplier, cost, schedule, and legal performance aspects. Searches out and investigates qualified suppliers and manufacturers. Develops new supply sources where needed. Leads the contracting effort, which may include the third-party procurement team, to establish the overall contract plan, proposal review criteria, and analysis and evaluation of proposals. Plans and leads negotiations with suppliers. Prepares contractual documents. Briefs senior management as required. May provide work leadership for lower-level employees.

Responsibilities: Conceive, develop, coordinate, implement, and manage contracts/procurements planned for assigned major programs, to optimize costs and ensure vendor/supplier performance. Lead the bid and proposal activity on new programs with contract content, preparing solicitations, and evaluating responses. Lead the review of contract requirements for determination of those clauses, which must be flowed down to the vendor/supplier. Ensure compliance with all import and export rules and regulations. Provide interpretation and leadership to ensure good business practices consistent with government and/or corporate and division policies and procedures. Ensure negotiations support the division's goals and enhance the division's competitive position.

Requirements: Requires 3 to 5 years' professional experience in procurement and/or contract/subcontract management and/or supply chain management. Also needed is a good understanding of e-procurement processes and systems. Knowledge of Oracle Financial system and Access is an asset as are excellent interpersonal and communication (verbal and written) skills and knowledge of/ experience with contract law.

Exhibit 8.5

COMPENSATION CONSULTANT ANNOUNCEMENT

Job Title: Executive Compensation Consultant
Location: Charlotte, North Carolina

Description: We are looking for bright, highly motivated individuals with hands-on experience in the design and implementation of compensation strategies and programs in a corporate environment or as a consultant. You will be managing the data collection, building databases, performing data analysis, and developing charts, graphs, tables, and other methods for displaying data and interpreting the results of the analysis for client reports. The successful candidate must be highly detail-oriented and have experience working independently and thinking critically about information and data.

Responsibilities: Resolve client executive and outside director compensation issues, specifically:

- Financial performance comparisons among client peer companies.
- Competitive pay analyses, including regression analysis and proxy research. (Familiarity with S&P's Research Insight is a plus).
- Short- and long-term incentive plan design.

Provide guidance and support to internal clients on a variety of tax and audit technical issues, including:

- Black-Scholes and binomial-option pricing models.
- Accounting and tax issues related to compensation programs.

Requirements: Candidate should have a bachelor's degree with a focus in economics, finance/business, accounting, or mathematic/statistics. Master's preferred. Must have 5+ years in a professional-services firm, preferably in a compensation environment, knowledge of Excel and PowerPoint, and demonstrated project management experience.

Exhibit 8.6

HR RECRUITER ANNOUNCEMENT

Job Title: Entry-Level HR Recruiter

Location: Phoenix, Arizona

Description: We're looking for a highly motivated, career-minded individual who will use creative sourcing and recruiting strategies to find and attract candidates for sales, marketing, administrative, and other positions for our in-house staff. A keen sense of urgency and excellent networking skills are required in this fast-paced, dynamic department. You'll have the opportunity to represent our company at college job fairs and other networking events. This is a great opportunity for candidates looking to use their corporate or agency recruiting experience. You'll be serving varied internal customers in editorial, art, sales, and our IT departments.

Requirements: Candidates should have a bachelor's in HR or business-related field, up to one year of recruiting experience (internships and co-ops will also be considered), strong written and verbal presentation skills, and the ability to manage competing priorities, often with compressed deadlines. Company provides a collaborative learning environment and exceptional benefits package that includes tuition reimbursement, company-paid healthcare, and 401(k) with matching program.

---

that each day must end with the job unfinished," she says. "But there are so many small successes each day, I have no problem leaving after a good eight-hour day." Sometimes she stays later, but only because she's engrossed in a project or talking to a candidate, not because the work requires it.

For her, the icing on the cake is looking around the company and seeing the results of her work: All the people she has brought in to help the company succeed. It's those people she meets and works with that make the difference. "I learn many things, not just about their work, but also about myself and how I operate in a variety of situations," Bramhall says. Whether it's because of her coworkers in HR, her managers, interviewees, or the people supporting her work internally, she comes away from each day with new insights about herself and the world.

Advice from Robyn Bramhall. Bramhall entered the field through the back door, so she doesn't encourage anyone to follow in her footsteps. The good news is that it doesn't take any special training to be a good recruiter; but it doesn't hurt to know something about a certain industry or type of work, especially if it involves technology. A good sense of equity, privacy, integrity, empathy, and humor also helps, she says.

Salaries vary greatly in recruiting. Bramhall was on a base-plus-commission plan at the agency, and she is now on a "base-plus-company bonus plus personal bonus plan." She made more at the agency she worked at before, but she wasn't happy, and the benefits were not as robust. "As a staff recruiter, you will not get rich, but you can make a comfortable living," she says.

Path 4: Banking, Finance, and Investment

A natural path for economics majors is a career in banking, finance, or investment. Within each sector, duties and responsibilities vary considerably, but each allows economics majors the chance to use the analytical skills they've honed in college.

Your Career Path

The choices for economics majors in banking and finance are as broad and rich as the field itself.

Banking

Although banks and other financial institutions generally fill higher-level positions from within, they do make management trainee programs available to college graduates. Economics majors tend to be particularly well prepared for these positions. These management trainee positions generally require individuals to spend some time working as a bank teller. But after showing aptitude and gaining some seniority, tellers with degrees in economics can go on to become bank managers and loan officers.

Financial institutions such as banks, savings and loan associations, credit unions, personal credit institutions, and finance companies may serve as depositories for cash and financial instruments and offer loans, investment counseling, consumer credit, trust management, and other financial services.

Some specialize in specific financial services. Financial managers in financial institutions include vice presidents, who may head one or more departments; bank branch managers; savings and loan association managers;

consumer credit managers; and credit union managers. These managers make decisions in accordance with policy set by the institution's board of directors and federal and state regulations.

Because of changing regulations and increased government scrutiny, managers in financial institutions must place greater emphasis on accurate reporting of financial data. They must have detailed knowledge of industries allied with banking, such as insurance, real estate, and securities, and a broad knowledge of business and industrial activities. With growing domestic and foreign competition, knowledge of an expanding and increasingly complex variety of financial services is becoming a necessity for managers in financial institutions and other corporations.

Besides supervising financial services, financial managers may advise individuals and businesses on financial planning.

Loan Officers and Loan Counselors.

Banks and other financial institutions need up-to-date information on companies and individuals applying for loans and credit. Customers and clients provide this information to the financial institution's loan officers and counselors, generally the first employees they see.

Loan officers prepare, analyze, and verify loan applications, make decisions regarding the extension of credit, and help borrowers fill out loan applications. Loan counselors help consumers with low income or a poor credit history qualify for credit, usually a home mortgage.

Loan officers usually specialize in commercial, consumer, or mortgage loans. Commercial or business loans help companies pay for new equipment or expand operations. Consumer loans include home equity, automobile, and personal loans. Mortgage loans are made to purchase real estate or to refinance existing mortgages.

Loan officers represent lending institutions; these institutions provide funds for a variety of purposes. Personal loans can be made to consolidate bills, purchase expensive items, such as cars or furniture, or finance college expenses.

Loan officers attempt to lower their firm's risk by obtaining collateral—security pledged for the payment of a loan. For example, when lending money for a college education, the bank may insist that the borrower offer his or her home as collateral. A borrower who is unable to repay the loan would have to sell the home to cover the loan. Loans backed by collateral also are beneficial to the customer because they generally carry lower interest rates.

Loan officers and counselors must keep abreast of new financial products and services so they can meet their customers' needs; for example, banks and other lenders now offer a variety of mortgage products, including reverse equity mortgages, shared equity mortgages, and adjustable rate mortgages. (For explanations of these mortgages, search Bankrate's website, www.bankrate.com.)

Loan officers meet with customers and gather basic information about the loan request. Often customers will not fully understand the information requested and will call the loan officer for assistance. Once the customer completes the financial forms, the loan officer begins to process them. The loan officer reviews the completed financial forms for accuracy and thoroughness and requests additional information if necessary. For example, the loan officer verifies that the customer has correctly identified the type and purpose of the loan. The loan officer then requests a credit report from one or more of the major credit reporting agencies. This information, along with comments from the loan officer, is included in a loan file and is compared with the lending institution's requirements. Banks and other lenders have established requirements for the maximum percentage of income that can safely go to repay loans. At this point, the loan officer, in conjunction with his or her manager, decides whether to grant the loan. A loan that would otherwise be denied may be approved if the customer can provide the lender appropriate collateral. The loan officer then informs the borrower of the decision, regardless of the outcome.

Loan counselors meet with consumers who are attempting to purchase a home or refinance debt, but who do not qualify for loans with banks. Often clients rely on income from self-employment or government assistance to prove that they can repay the loan. Counselors also help to psychologically prepare consumers to be homeowners and to pay their debts. Counselors frequently work with clients who have little or no experience with financial matters.

Loan counselors provide positive reinforcement along with the financial tools needed to qualify for a loan. This assistance may take several forms. Occasionally, counselors simply need to explain to the client or customer what information loan officers need to complete a loan transaction. Most of the time, loan counselors help clients qualify for a bank-financed mortgage loan. The loan counselor helps the client complete an application and researches federal, state, and local government programs that could provide the money needed for the client to purchase the home. Often, several government programs are combined to provide the necessary money.

Loan officers and counselors usually work in offices, but mortgage loan officers frequently move from office to office and often visit homes of clients while completing a loan request. Commercial loan officers employed by large firms may travel frequently to prepare complex loan agreements.

Most loan officers and counselors work a standard forty-hour week but may work longer, particularly mortgage loan officers who are free to take on as many customers as they choose. Loan officers and counselors usually carry a heavy caseload and sometimes cannot accept new clients until they complete current cases. They are especially busy when interest rates are low, which results in a surge in loan applications.

Finance

Practically every firm—whether in manufacturing, communications, finance, education, or health care—has at least one financial manager. They may be treasurers, controllers, credit managers, or cash managers; they prepare the financial reports required by the firm to conduct its operations and to ensure that the firm satisfies tax and regulatory requirements. Financial managers also oversee the flow of cash and financial instruments, monitor the extension of credit, assess the risk of transactions, raise capital, analyze investments, develop information to assess the present and future financial status of the firm, and communicate with stockholders and other investors.

In small firms, chief financial officers usually handle all financial management functions. However, in large firms these officers oversee financial management departments and help top managers develop financial and economic policy and establish procedures, delegate authority, and oversee the implementation of these policies.

Highly trained and experienced financial managers head each financial department. Controllers direct the preparation of all financial reports—income statements, balance sheets, and special reports, such as depreciation schedules. They also oversee the accounting, audit, or budget departments.

Cash and credit managers monitor and control the flow of cash receipts and disbursements to meet the business and investment needs of the firm. For example, cash flow projections are needed to determine whether loans must be obtained to meet cash requirements, or whether surplus cash may be invested in interest-bearing instruments.

Risk and insurance managers oversee programs to minimize risks and losses that may arise from financial transactions and business operations undertaken by the institution. Credit operations managers establish credit rating criteria, determine credit ceilings, and monitor their institution's extension of credit.

Reserve officers review their institution's financial statements and direct the purchase and sale of bonds and other securities to maintain the asset-liability ratio required by law.

User representatives in international accounting develop integrated international financial and accounting systems for the banking transactions of multinational organizations. A working knowledge of the financial systems of foreign countries is essential.

Investment

Brokers and Investors. Typically, individuals in positions in brokerage and investment firms provide investment advice to individuals and businesses.

Stockbrokers or traders are also called securities sales representatives, registered representatives, or account executives. And most investors, whether they are individuals with a few hundred dollars to invest or large institutions with millions, turn to these professionals when buying or selling stocks, bonds, shares in mutual funds, insurance annuities, or other financial products.

When an investor wishes to buy or sell securities, sales representatives may relay the order through their firms' offices to the floor of a securities exchange, such as the New York Stock Exchange. There, securities sales representatives known as brokers' floor representatives buy and sell securities. If a security is not traded on an exchange, the sales representative sends the order to the firm's trading department, where a security trader trades it directly with a dealer in an over-the-counter market, such as the NASDAQ computerized trading system. After the transaction has been completed, the sales representative notifies the customer of the final price.

Securities sales representatives also provide many related services for their customers. Depending on a customer's knowledge of the market, they may explain the meaning of stock market terms and trading practices; offer financial counseling; devise an individual financial portfolio for the client, including securities, life insurance, corporate and municipal bonds, mutual funds, certificates of deposit, annuities, and other investments; and offer advice on the purchase or sale of particular securities.

Not all customers have the same investment goals. Some individuals may prefer long-term investments designed either for capital growth or to provide income over the years; others might want to invest in speculative securities that they hope will rise in price quickly. Securities sales representatives furnish information about the advantages and disadvantages of an investment based on each person's objectives. They also supply the latest price quotations on any security in which the investor is interested, as well as information on the activities and financial positions of the corporations issuing these securities.

Most securities sales representatives serve individual investors, but others specialize in institutional investors. In institutional investing, most sales representatives concentrate on a specific financial product, such as stocks, bonds, options, annuities, or commodities futures. Some handle the sale of new issues, such as corporate securities issued to finance plant expansion.

The most important part of a sales representative's job is finding clients and building a customer base. Thus, beginning securities sales representatives spend much of their time searching for customers, relying heavily on cold calls. They may meet some clients through business and social contacts. Many sales representatives find it useful to get additional exposure by teaching adult education investment courses or by giving lectures at libraries or social clubs. Brokerage firms may give sales representatives lists of people with whom the firm has done business in the past. Sometimes sales representatives may inherit the clients of representatives who have retired.

Financial services sales representatives sell banking and related services. They contact potential customers to explain their services and to learn the customers' banking and other financial needs. They may discuss services such as deposit accounts, lines of credit, sales or inventory financing, certificates of deposit, cash management, or investment services. They may solicit businesses to participate in consumer credit card programs.

At most small- and medium-size banks, branch managers and commercial loan officers are responsible for marketing the bank's financial services. As banks offer more and increasingly complex financial services—for example, securities brokerage and financial planning—the job of the financial services sales representative has assumed greater importance.

Financial planners develop and implement financial plans for individuals and businesses using their knowledge of tax and investment strategies, securities, insurance, pension plans, and real estate. Planners interview clients to determine their assets, liabilities, cash flow, insurance coverage, tax status, and financial objectives. All this information is then analyzed and a financial plan is developed and tailored to each client's needs.

Securities sales representatives usually work in offices where there is a lot of activity. They continually check the prices of securities, and when sales activity increases, due perhaps to unanticipated changes in the economy, the pace may become very hectic. Established securities sales representatives usually work the same hours as others in the business community. Beginners who are seeking customers may work much longer hours, however. Most securities sales representatives accommodate customers by meeting with them in the evenings or on weekends.

Financial services sales representatives normally work in a comfortable, less stressful office environment. They generally work forty hours a week. They may, however, spend considerable time outside the office meeting with present and prospective clients, attending civic functions, and participating in trade association meetings. Some financial services sales representatives work exclusively inside banks providing service to walk-in customers.

Brokerage Clerks. Brokerage clerks work behind the scenes to produce records associated with financial transactions. Brokerage clerks, who work in the operations areas of securities firms, perform many duties to facilitate the sale and purchase of stocks, bonds, commodities, and other kinds of investments. These clerks produce the necessary records of all transactions that occur in their area of the business.

Job titles depend upon the type of work performed. Purchase-and-sale clerks match orders to buy with orders to sell. They balance and verify stock trades by comparing the records of the selling firm to those of the buying firm. Dividend clerks ensure timely payments of stock or cash dividends to clients of a particular brokerage firm. Transfer clerks execute customer requests for changes to security registration and examine stock certificates for adherence to banking regulations. Receive-and-deliver clerks facilitate the receipt and delivery of securities among firms and institutions. Margin clerks post accounts and monitor activity in customers' accounts. Their job is to ensure that customers make their payments and stay within legal boundaries concerning stock purchases.

A significant and growing number of brokerage clerks use custom-designed software programs to process transactions, which enables transactions to be processed faster than if they were done manually. Only a few customized accounts are still handled manually.

Preparing for the Work

Training for Bank Tellers and Clerks

When hiring tellers and clerks, banks seek applicants who enjoy public contact and have good numerical, clerical, and communication skills. Tellers must feel comfortable handling large amounts of cash and working with computers and video terminals, because their work is highly automated. In some metropolitan areas, employers seek multilingual tellers.

Although tellers and clerks work independently, their record keeping is closely supervised. Accuracy and attention to detail are vital.

Tellers should be courteous, attentive, and patient in dealing with the public, because customers often judge a bank by the way they are treated at the teller window. Maturity, tact, and the ability to quickly explain bank procedures and services are important in helping customers complete transactions or make financial decisions.

Many entrants transfer from other occupations; virtually all have at least a high school education. In general, banks prefer applicants who have had high school courses in mathematics, accounting, bookkeeping, economics, and public speaking.

New tellers and clerks at larger banks receive at least one week of formal classroom training. Formal training is followed by several weeks of on-the-job training, during which tellers observe experienced workers before doing the work themselves.

Smaller banks rely primarily upon on-the-job training. In addition to instruction in basic duties, many banks now include extensive training in the bank's products and services so that tellers can refer customers to appropriate products, communication and sales skills, and instruction on equipment such as ATMs and on-line video terminals.

In large banks, beginners usually start as limited-transaction tellers, cashing checks and processing simple transactions for a few days, before becoming full-service tellers. Often banks simultaneously train tellers for other clerical duties.

Advancement opportunities are good for well-trained, motivated employees. Experienced tellers may advance to head teller, customer service representative, or new accounts clerk. Outstanding tellers who have college degrees or specialized training offered by the banking industry may be promoted to managerial positions.

Banks encourage this upward mobility by providing access to education and other sources of additional training. College graduates with degrees in economics, finance, business, or related fields may participate in management trainee programs.

Tellers can prepare for better jobs by taking courses offered or accredited by the American Institute of Banking, an educational affiliate of the American Bankers Association (aba.com/Conferences+and+Education/aib_main. htm). These organizations have several hundred chapters in cities across the country and numerous study groups in small communities, and they offer correspondence courses. They also work closely with local colleges and universities in preparing courses of study. Most banks *collaborate with these schools*, which assist local banks in conducting cooperative training programs or developing independent training programs.

In addition, many banks reimburse employees for college tuition after successful completion of their courses. Although most courses are meant for employed tellers, some community colleges offer preemployment training programs. These programs can help prepare applicants for jobs in banking and can give them an advantage over other job seekers.

Training for Finance Careers

A bachelor's degree in economics, accounting, or finance, or in business administration with an emphasis on accounting or finance, is the minimum academic preparation for financial managers. However, a master's of business administration (MBA) degree is the gold standard. Many financial management positions are filled by promoting experienced, technically skilled professional personnel—for example, accountants, budget analysts, credit analysts, insurance analysts, loan officers, and securities analysts—or accounting or related department supervisors in large institutions.

Because of the growing complexity of global trade, shifting federal and state laws and regulations, and a proliferation of complex financial instruments, continuing education is becoming vital for financial managers. Firms often provide opportunities for workers to broaden their knowledge and skills and encourage employees to take graduate courses at colleges and universities or attend conferences sponsored by the company.

In addition, financial management, banking, and credit union associations, often in cooperation with colleges and universities, sponsor numerous national and local training programs. People enrolled prepare extensively at home and then attend sessions on subjects such as accounting management, budget management, corporate cash management, financial analysis, international banking, and data-processing and management information systems. Many firms pay all or part of the costs for those who successfully complete courses. Although experience, ability, and leadership are emphasized for promotion, advancement may be accelerated by this type of special study.

In some cases, financial managers may also broaden their skills and exhibit their competency in specialized fields by attaining professional certification. For example, the CFA Institute (cfainstitute.org) confers the Chartered Financial Analyst designation on investment professionals who earn bachelor's degrees, pass three test levels, and have three or more years of experience in the field.

The National Association of Credit Management (nacm.org) administers a three-part certification program for business credit professionals. Through a combination of experience and examinations, these financial managers pass through the level of Credit Business Associate to Credit Business Fellow to Certified Credit Executive.

The Association for Finance Professionals (afponline.org) offers the Certified Treasury Professional and Certified Treasury Professional Associate designations to distinguish financial professionals with expertise in risk management, capital structure, corporate governance, and mergers and acquisitions as well as cash management.

Individuals interested in becoming financial managers should enjoy working independently, dealing with people, and analyzing detailed account information. The ability to communicate effectively, both verbally and in writing, is also important. They also need tact, good judgment, and the ability to establish effective personal relationships to oversee staff.

Financial analysis and management have been revolutionized by technological improvements in personal computers and data-processing equipment. Knowledge of these applications is vital to upgrade managerial skills and to enhance advancement opportunities.

Because financial management is critical for efficient business operations, well-trained, experienced financial managers who display a strong grasp of the operations of various departments within their organization are prime candidates for promotion to top management positions.

Some financial managers transfer to closely related positions in other industries. Those with extensive experience and access to sufficient capital may head their own consulting firms.

Training for Careers in Brokerage and Investment Firms

Because securities sales representatives must be well informed about economic conditions and trends, a college education is seen as essential, especially in the larger securities firms. In fact, the overwhelming majority of workers in this occupation are college graduates. Although employers seldom require specialized academic training, courses in business administration, economics, and finance are helpful.

The financial scandals surrounding Enron and the subsequent passage of the Sarbanes-Oxley Act of 2002 have ushered in a new era of corporate accountability, ethical standards, and accuracy and transparency in financial statements. While much of the responsibility for complying with this new raft of regulation falls on CFOs and certain specialists, the atmosphere is different for everyone. Companies expect above-board behavior, candor, and strict adherence to the law from top to bottom.

Many employers consider personal qualities and skills more important than academic training. Employers seek applicants who have sales ability and good communication skills, are well groomed, and possess a strong desire to succeed. Self-confidence and an ability to handle frequent rejections also are important ingredients for success.

Because maturity and the ability to work independently also are important, many employers prefer to hire those who have achieved success in other jobs. Some firms prefer candidates with sales experience, particularly those who have worked on commission in areas such as real estate or insurance. Therefore, most entrants to this occupation transfer from other jobs. Some begin working as securities sales representatives following retirement from other fields.

Securities sales representatives must meet state licensing requirements, which generally include passing an examination and, in some cases, furnishing a personal bond. In addition, sales representatives must register as representatives of their firm according to regulations of the securities exchanges where they do business or the National Association of Securities Dealers, Inc. (nasd.com).

Before beginners can qualify as registered representatives, they must pass the General Securities Registered Representative Examination, administered by the NASD, and be an employee of a registered firm for at least four months. Most states require a second examination—the Uniform Securities Agents State Law Examination. These tests measure the prospective representative's knowledge of the securities business, customer protection requirements, and record-keeping procedures. Many take correspondence courses in preparation for the securities examinations.

Most employers provide on-the-job training to help securities sales representatives meet the requirements for registration. In most firms, the training period generally takes about four months. Trainees in large firms may receive classroom instruction in securities analysis, effective speaking, and the finer points of selling; take courses offered by business schools and associations; and undergo a period of on-the-job training lasting up to two years.

Many firms like to rotate their trainees among various departments in the firm to give them a broader perspective of the securities business. In small firms, sales representatives generally receive training in outside institutions and on the job.

Securities sales representatives must understand the basic characteristics of a wide variety of financial products offered by brokerage firms. Representatives periodically take training, through their firms or outside institutions, to keep abreast of new financial products as they are introduced on the market and to improve their sales techniques. Training in the use of computers is important because the securities sales business is highly automated.

The principal form of advancement for securities sales representatives is an increase in the number and size of the accounts they handle. Although beginners usually service the accounts of individual investors, eventually they may handle very large institutional accounts such as those of banks and pension funds. Some experienced sales representatives become branch office managers and supervise other sales representatives while continuing to provide services for their own customers. A few representatives advance to top management positions or become partners in their firms.

Banks and other credit institutions prefer to hire college graduates for financial services sales jobs. A business administration degree with a specialization in finance or a liberal arts degree including courses in accounting, economics, and marketing serves as excellent preparation for this job.

Financial services sales representatives learn through on-the-job training under the supervision of bank officers. Outstanding performance can lead to promotion to managerial positions.

Some brokerage clerk entrants are college graduates with degrees in business, finance, or the liberal arts. Some brokerage firms have a set plan of advancement that tracks college graduates from entry-level clerk jobs to management positions. These workers may start at higher salaries and advance more rapidly than those without degrees.

Career Outlook

Bank Tellers

Bank tellers will see a slight drop in employment through 2014. More and more customers are banking online or by phone and are using ATMs and automated kiosks instead of tellers to conduct transactions. A few years ago, banks were even shuttering locations and pushing customers toward these cheaper alternatives. However, banks are also adding more neighborhood branches and expanding their hours of service to enhance convenience and win more customers. That trend, combined with the high turnover associated with teller positions, should mean ample opportunities. Tellers who have excellent customer service skills, are knowledgeable about a variety of financial services and can sell those services will be in greater demand in the future.

Employment of tellers also is being affected by the increasing use of twenty-four-hour telephone centers by many large banks. These centers allow a customer to interact with a bank representative at a distant location, either by telephone or by video terminal. Such centers usually are staffed by customer service representatives, who can handle a wider variety of transactions than tellers can, including applications for loans and credit cards.

Loan Officers and Counselors

Employment of loan officers and counselors is expected to grow more slowly than the average for all occupations through 2014. College graduates and those with banking, lending, or sales experience should have the best job prospects. Employment growth stemming from economic expansion and population increases—which generate demand for loans—will be partially offset by increased automation that speeds lending processes and by the increasing number of online loan applications. Job opportunities for loan officers are influenced by the volume of applications, which is determined largely by interest rates and by the overall level of economic activity.

The use of credit scoring has made the loan evaluation process much simpler than in the past and even unnecessary in some cases. Credit scoring allows loan officers—particularly loan underwriters—to evaluate many more loans in much less time, thus increasing the loan officer's efficiency. In addition, the mortgage application process has become highly automated and standardized, a simplification that has enabled online mortgage loan vendors to offer their services over the Internet. Online vendors accept loan applications from customers online and determine which lenders have the best interest rates for particular loans.

Although loans remain a major source of revenue for banks, demand for new loans fluctuates and affects the income and employment opportunities of loan officers. An upswing in the economy or a decline in interest rates often results in a surge in real estate buying and mortgage refinancing, requiring loan officers to work long hours processing applications and inducing lenders to hire additional loan officers, who often are paid by commission on the value of the loans they place. When the real estate market slows, loan officers often suffer a decline in earnings and may even be subject to layoffs. The same applies to commercial loan officers, whose workloads increase during good economic times as companies seek to invest more in their businesses. In difficult economic conditions, an increase in the number of delinquent loans results in more demand for loan collection officers.

Financial Managers

Like other managerial occupations, the number of applicants for financial management positions is expected to exceed the number of openings, resulting in competition for jobs. Those with lending experience and familiarity with the latest lending regulations and financial products and services should enjoy the best opportunities for branch management jobs in banks. Those with a graduate degree, a strong analytical background, and knowledge of various aspects of financial management, such as asset management and information and technology management, should enjoy the best opportunities for other financial management positions. Developing expertise in a rapidly growing industry, such as health care, could also be an advantage in the job market.

Employment of financial managers is expected to increase about as fast as the average for all occupations through 2014. The increasing need for financial expertise as a result of regulatory reforms and the expansion of the economy will drive job growth over the next decade. Many firms have reduced the ranks of middle managers in an effort to be more efficient and competitive, but much of the downsizing and restructuring is complete.

Securities Sales Representatives

Because of the highly competitive nature of securities sales work, many beginners leave the occupation because they are unable to establish a sufficient clientele. Once established, however, securities sales representatives have a very strong attachment to their occupation because of high earnings and the considerable investment in training.

The demand for securities sales representatives fluctuates as the economy expands and contracts. Thus, in an economic downturn the number of people seeking jobs usually exceeds the number of openings—sometimes by a great deal. Even during periods of rapid economic expansion, competition for securities sales training positions—particularly in larger firms—is keen because of potentially high earnings.

Job opportunities for both securities and financial services sales representatives should be best for mature individuals with successful work experience. Opportunities for inexperienced sales representatives should be best in smaller firms.

Employment of securities sales representatives is expected to grow about as fast as average for all occupations through 2014. Employment of financial services sales agents in banks will increase as banks expand their product offerings in order to compete directly with other investment firms.

Baby boomers in their peak savings years will fuel much of this increase in investment. Saving for retirement has been made much easier by the government, which continues to offer a number of tax-favorable pension plans, such as the 401(k) and the Roth IRA. The participation of more women in the workforce also means higher household incomes and more women qualifying for pensions. Many of these pensions are self-directed, meaning that the recipient has the responsibility for investing the money. With such large amounts of money to invest, sales agents, in their role as financial advisors, will be in great demand.

Other factors that will affect the demand for brokers are the increasing number and complexity of investment products, as well as the effects of globalization. As the public and businesses become more sophisticated about investing, they are venturing into the options and futures markets. Brokers are needed to buy or sell these products, which are not traded online. Also, markets for investment are expanding with the increase in global trading of stocks and bonds. Furthermore, the New York Stock Exchange has extended its trading hours to accommodate trading in foreign stocks and compete with foreign exchanges.

Brokerage Clerks

Employment of brokerage clerks is expected to grow more slowly than average for all occupations through 2014. With people increasingly investing in securities, brokerage clerks will be required to process larger volumes of transactions. Moreover, some brokerage clerks will still be needed to update records, enter changes into customers' accounts, and verify transfers of securities. However, the emergence of online trading and widespread automation in the securities and commodities industry will limit demand for brokerage clerks in the coming decade.

Salaries

Bank Tellers
The median annual income for full-time tellers in 2004 was $21,120. The lowest 10 percent earned less than $15,850, while the top 10 percent earned more than $28,100. Some banks offer incentives, whereby tellers earn supplemental rewards for inducing customers to use other financial products and services offered by the bank. In general, greater responsibilities result in a higher salary. Experience, length of service, and, especially, the location and size of the bank also are important. Part-time tellers generally do not receive typical benefits, such as life and health insurance.

Loan Officers
The form of compensation for loan officers varies, depending on the lending institution. Some banks offer salary plus commission as an incentive to increase the number of loans processed, while others pay only salaries. Loan officers who are paid on a commission basis usually earn more than those on salary only and those who work for smaller banks generally earn less than those employed by larger institutions. Earnings of loan officers with graduate degrees or professional certifications are higher.

In 2004, median annual earnings for loan officers were $48,830. Loan officers working in the executive branch of the federal government and those with accounting, tax preparation, bookkeeping, and payroll services had among the highest median incomes. According to a 2005 salary survey conducted by Robert Half International, a staffing services firm specializing in accounting and finance, consumer loan officers with one to three years of experience earned between $30,000 and $35,000 in 2005; commercial loan officers with one to three years of experience earned between $45,500 and $70,000. Consumer loan officers with more than three years of experience earned between $25,500 and $50,000; commercial loan officers with more than three years of experience earned between $61,750 and $100,000. Banks and other lenders also sometimes offer their loan officers free checking privileges and somewhat lower interest rates on personal loans.

Financial Managers
The median annual salary of financial managers was $81,880 in 2004. The lowest 10 percent earned $59,490 or less, while the top 10 percent earned more than $112,320. Those handling securities and commodity contracts

intermediation and brokerage had the highest median incomes—nearly $130,000.

According to another 2005 survey by Robert Half International, directors of finance earned between $78,500 and $178,250, and corporate controllers earned between $61,250 and $147,250. A 2004 survey conducted by Abbot, Langer, and Associates, Inc., a human resources management consulting firm, reported the following median annual incomes:

Chief corporate financial officers	$130,000
Corporate controllers	$86,150
Cost accounting managers	$67,161
General accounting managers	$64,100

A 2004 survey conducted by Mercer Human Resource Consulting revealed the following cash earnings for top finance and accounting executives:

Chief financial officer	$360,700
Corporate treasurer	$217,000
Top corporate tax executive	$195,100
Corporate controller	$159,500
Top corporate audit executive	$161,200
Top corporate accounting executive	$150,300
Senior accountant	$56,000
Intermediate financial analyst	$52,500

Salary levels depend upon the manager's experience and the size and location of the organization and is likely to be higher in larger organizations and cities. Many financial managers in private industry receive additional compensation in the form of bonuses, which also vary substantially by the size of the firm.

Securities and Financial Services Sales Representatives
Media annual earnings of securities and financial services sales representatives for 2004 were $69,200; the middle 50 percent earned between $40,750 and $131,290. On average, financial services sales representatives earn considerably less than securities sales representatives.

Trainees usually are paid an hourly wage or salary, until they meet licensing and registration requirements. After candidates are licensed and registered, their earnings depend on commissions from the sale or purchase of stocks and bonds, life insurance, or other securities for customers. Commission earnings are likely to be high when there is much buying and selling and low when there is a slump in market activity.

Most firms provide sales representatives with a steady income by paying a "draw against commission"—a minimum salary based on commissions that they can be expected to earn. Securities sales representatives who can provide their clients with the most complete financial services should enjoy the greatest income stability.

Brokers who work for discount brokerage firms that promote trading by phone and online are usually paid a salary, sometimes boosted by bonuses based on the office's profitability. Financial services sales representatives usually are paid a salary, but bonuses and commissions are now accounting for a larger portion of their income.

Brokerage Clerks

Salaries for brokerage clerks vary considerably, depending upon the region of the country and the size of the firm. Median hourly earnings in 2004 were $16.94, which corresponds to $33,880 based on forty-hour weeks. The middle 50 percent fell between $13.52 per hour ($27,040) and $21.60 per hour ($43,200).

Exhibit 9.1
ECONOMIST ANNOUNCEMENT

Job Title: International Financial Analyst
Location: Chicago, Illinois

Description: Fortune 500 company is seeking an experienced financial analyst to support company's growing international markets, particularly South America and China. Position will focus on new ventures, capital projects, budgeting/forecasting, and modeling. Interacts with various international business units' management.

Requirements: Candidate should have 5 to 10 years experience with a strong preference in the international arena. In addition to financial planning experience, the candidate should have a solid accounting knowledge/ foundation. MBA a plus. Candidate should have excellent project-management skills, capital investment, and quantitative analysis experience. Bilingual in Spanish or Mandarin a plus. Interpersonal skills key. Good career opportunities and benefits. Salary $70,000 to $95,000.

Exhibit 9.2
STATISTICAL ANALYST ANNOUNCEMENT

Job Title: Statistical Analyst
Location: Portsmouth, New Hampshire

Description: Under minimal supervision, ensures more complex regulatory bureau filings are in compliance with state regulators, insurance divisions and commissioners mandating new rating requirements, informational needs, and financial reporting requirements. Responsible for integrity of company's coding structure by ensuring quality of data in various corporate systems. Provide formal guidance and direction to less experienced analysts by assisting with orientation and ongoing development, answering questions, and serving in a lead capacity.

Requirements: Bachelor's degree or equivalent plus 4 to 6 years' insurance experience. Thorough knowledge and understanding of property and casualty insurance, insurance company operations, state insurance laws, and regulations affecting insurance practices. Effectively manage multiple concurrent objectives and/or activities. Effective judgment in prioritizing and time allocation. Advanced analytical, problem solving, and organizational skills. Demonstrated ability to use spreadsheet, data base software, and Microsoft applications. Demonstrated ability to influence and negotiate effectively.

Comprehensive benefits package, including life insurance, tuition reimbursement, and work/life resources.

Sample Job Ads

To give you an idea of the kind of positions available, examine the sample job announcements in Exhibits 9.1 through 9.7.

Close-Ups

J. Douglas Nobles, Loan Officer/President
J. Douglas Nobles works at the Mortgage Shop, a branch of Lamar Bank in Hattiesburg, Mississippi. Before that, he worked as the manager/loan officer of

Exhibit 9.3
FINANCIAL SERVICES REPRESENTATIVE ANNOUNCEMENT

Job Title: Financial Services Representative
Location: New York City

Description: An entry-level position with a Wall Street firm in the field of financial services. We offer a complete training program for qualified candidates, with the potential to advance in management. We work with clients one on one to help them achieve their financial goals, such as retirement, education, reducing taxes, or the accumulation of wealth.

Requirements: Bachelor's in business or economics. We will train you for your securities licensing exams and teach you about the many products and services that we offer, as well as about the compliance and regulatory aspects of the investment industry. Our continuing and advanced education includes ongoing training in investment sales and management techniques. No experience necessary—all you need is the willingness to learn the business and a strong commitment to professional service. Representatives have gone on to successful careers in management.

United Companies Financial Corporation in Hattiesburg for seventeen years. He started out collecting loan payments, then advanced to assistant manager and loan officer at United, where he eventually ran the Hattiesburg office.

Though the career path is different from when he started, Nobles feels the spirit is the same. There's no getting around working with people when you're a loan officer, and it's one of the main reasons he entered the field. "Certain fields are right for certain people, and banking has always been something that I enjoyed doing," he says. "I've always enjoyed helping people, and in banking you're able to provide much-needed assistance to your customers."

On the Job. Larger banks often have extensive training programs to bring their new hires up to speed. Many train their employees for six to eight weeks before transitioning them into their formal roles. These programs basically walk a new officer through each and every branch of the bank to give them

Exhibit 9.4
FINANCIAL ANALYSIS SPECIALIST ANNOUNCEMENT

Job Title: Financial Analysis Specialist
Location: Glendale, California

Description: Responsible for analysis and interpretation of financial information. Utilizing independent judgment and discretion, identifies trends, variances, and key issues and provides recommendations for adjustment. Responsible for conducting moderate to complex financial analysis projects and/or reporting. Prepares financial reports and recommends improvements in financial reporting systems. May conduct audits to ensure financial controls are maintained. Responsible for achieving unit cost objectives for provider contracts managed on a national basis. These include leased networks and the analysis of other areas where national initiatives could benefit overall unit cost. Responsible for supporting the development of strategic goals and managing/developing the analytical framework to achieve results. Working with the local contracting team and other key personnel, perform effective analyses on assigned contracts and determine ROI and risk trade-offs on the proposed contracting strategies. Identification and communication of areas of cost reduction opportunities. Communication and influencing of the negotiation process to ensure goals and targets are met.

Requirements: Bachelor's degree in finance or a related field and three to five years of financial analysis in the insurance or managed care industry or related experience. Risk management/investment banking/mergers and acquisition experience a plus. General knowledge of insurance products, procedures, and systems for specific functional area. Requires strong negotiation skills and business maturity to achieve optimal balance between competing priorities of earnings and growth. Knowledge of both the indemnity and managed care market, including product offerings, HMO regulatory environment, competitor offerings, provider contracts, and the dynamics of the retail sales/enrollment process a plus.

a good overall view of the bank itself. Still, much of the training comes on the job. Nobles says that even a new arrival with a bachelor's or a master's degree will get most of his or her training in this way. "Each bank does things a little differently, and each type of loan is handled a little differently," he says. "It's a matter of working on the job to learn the differences."

Exhibit 9.5

LOAN OFFICER ANNOUNCEMENT

Job Title: Loan Officer
Location: Las Vegas, Nevada

Description: As a loan officer for a financial services firm with more than $1 trillion in assets, you will solicit mortgage loans from referral sources. Those sources include, but are not limited to, Realtors, builders, and other networking avenues. You will take complete applications for mortgage loans, including follow-up for documentation required for processing in accordance with corporate policies and procedures, keep all parties to the transaction informed as to status of application, set the customers'/sources' expectations, educate them on the entire mortgage origination process, quote rates to customers, and follow through to ensure the loan is properly locked. It is preferred that you maintain a minimum monthly pipeline of $500,000. You will provide a high level of customer service, comply with all federal and state policies, and adhere to all HMDA requirements.

Qualifications: Minimum three years of mortgage lending or mortgage banking experience and bachelor's degree or 4 years' equivalent work experience in sales and/or real estate. Sales and consulting skills required. Excellent written and oral communication skills. Knowledge of real estate market in local area. Knowledge of FHA, VA, FNMA, FHLMC guidelines. FHA/VA sales experience preferred. Intermediate PC skills required.

Seminars are another way to improve service. The banking industry, fortunately, is excellent about providing periodic training in new banking laws and procedures.

Once new loan officers ease into their full-time positions, they can expect to spend a lot of time on the phone and discussing finances with customers in their offices. Nobles helps people who are financially stressed to work out solutions to get them back in good financial standing. He helps them lower their total financial obligations by using equity in their home or reduce their payments to better handle their obligations. He also takes credit applications, spends time visiting different properties that people want to borrow money on, and so forth.

Exhibit 9.6
CREDIT MANAGER ANNOUNCEMENT

Job Title: Credit Manager
Location: Annapolis, Maryland

Description: Excellent opportunity for a strong credit manager to join a national distribution company. This position's primary responsibility will be credit analysis and extending credit to small businesses with less than $30 million in revenue. Secondary responsibilities include assisting the sales force and overseeing collections. Due to the high volume and low profit margin nature of the business, the ideal candidate's background will have a heavy emphasis on credit analysis, not collections.

Requirements: Qualified candidates will have 7+ years' credit and/or financial analysis evaluating the creditworthiness of small businesses. Must have strong leadership, managerial, and communication skills. Bachelor's degree and/or CCE preferred.

Exhibit 9.7
FINANCIAL PLANNER ANNOUNCEMENT

Job Title: Financial Advisor/Financial Planner
Location: Boulder, Colorado

Description: A premier financial services company, we are one of the nation's most enduring mutual fund/financial planning firms. Our focus is long-term, one-on-one relationships in which our financial advisors and staff members interact with clients in the communities where they live. As a financial advisor, your responsibilities will include targeting prospective clients, identifying their needs, recommending appropriate solutions, helping them take action on your recommendations and providing personal client service. While you pursue a career as a financial advisor, we provide the means, the tools, processes, support systems, and products to assist you in achieving the goals you have set for yourself, your clients, and your business.

Requirements: Some requirements are strong sales and/or people skills, a genuine desire to help others, an interest in learning financial planning methods, and a personal commitment to becoming a professional in the financial services business.

Nobles bird-dogs potential customers by calling on lenders that don't do the type of business that the Mortgage Shop does to get them to refer their business to him. The job, he says, is basically a sales job—selling the loan packages that they have in order to help someone out of a financial bind.

The work can be sporadic. In slower times, he solicits new business or completes paperwork. There's a lot of paperwork. Nobles works at least forty hours a week, and sometimes more, though he does operate in a relaxed atmosphere. "Some banks make you feel that they are too important to talk to you and too important to help you out," Nobles says. "We don't do that. We try to make our customers feel they are very important. By doing so, they'll recommend us to other customers, and they'll come back when they need more financial assistance. You have to be personable and friendly in this business to make it."

Nobles says he's been in the business long enough to know how he can help each customer, and it's always a challenge for him to make it work, especially with people from all types of backgrounds. His least favorite task is failing in finding an investor to take on a loan and having to turn down the customer. There are just no words to sweeten that kind of news and help a person save face.

Advice from J. Douglas Nobles.

Advice from J. Douglas Nobles. Nobles suggests getting a bachelor of science in banking and finance or banking and real estate. A strong knowledge of the banking and real estate industries is important, but personality can be the deciding factor. You must be friendly, willing to spend time with your customers, and able to put them at ease. You have to be able to listen to people's problems and empathize with them.

Be prepared to start at the bottom, work hard, and work your way up. Learn as much as you can. Listen to the experts in the field. Be friendly to everyone you meet. "You never know when that person might need your help," Nobles says.

Finally, get on the level of your customers. "Don't give them the impression that you're too good to talk to them," he says. "Instead, become their friend. You'll spend a lot of time talking, but in the end, it will pay off."

Richard G. Leader, Executive Director, Institutional Sales

Richard G. Leader is an executive director with CIBC Oppenheimer, an investment broker in Houston, Texas. He earned a B.A. from Wake Forest in Winston-Salem, North Carolina, and an M.B.A. from Vanderbilt University in Nashville, Tennessee. He is also a C.F.A. (Chartered Financial Analyst) and has been working in the field for twenty years.

Leader started by investing some of the savings from his paper route in the stock market at the age of twelve. His first stock went up 50 percent in a year, and he's been hooked ever since. His mother took him to an annual meeting at General Motors when he was fourteen. "This made me realize that stocks represent interests in real operating businesses, not just meaningless or speculative price quotes," he says.

His first real job came as he was finishing his M.B.A. He blanketed Wall Street with letters and drummed up a few interviews. Those translated into three offers and a job at Citibank's Investment Management Group. He later got transferred to Houston and left Citibank to work for a series of firms, culminating in his job with Oppenheimer.

The term institutional sales in Leader's job title translates to selling a brokerage firm's products and services to professional money managers, such as mutual funds, pension, and retirement funds. Anyone with a few million dollars, even wealthy individuals, might qualify as an institution.

On the Job. Leader is constantly looking for information or ideas that will beat the market. "If you can't beat the market, you might as well buy an index," he says. Ideas usually come from one of Oppenhemier's industry analysts, who are experts in areas of business such as autos, aluminum, semiconductors, and telecommunications. Leader then gets information that the analysts believe is correct, such as improved earnings prospects for a company and persuades customers to buy large quantities of that stock through the firm—earning a commission for the seller in the process. (Leader works on 100 percent commission.) If he's right more often than he's wrong, clients gain confidence in Leader and Oppenheimer, and they do more business with them over time.

In addition to research sales, Oppenheimer also sells new issues of public stock, or IPOs—initial public offerings. This can be extraordinarily easy or difficult depending on market conditions and how hot an industry is. For example, one recent IPO was up 100 percent the very first day. "That was an easy sale," Leader says. "We really 'gave' that stock to only our very best customers."

Leader earns more than $300,000 a year, which reflects his vast network of contacts and experience in the business. When you first join a firm, you have a small customer base based on cold calls or family connections. As your customer base increases and as their assets increase, your commission increases. Some firms give a base salary for a year or two for their beginning salespeople—which is usually modest at best, just something to keep the pantry full.

Competition, both for clients and in the market, is heated. Most big institutions deal with twenty-five or more brokers, each trying to have his or her voice heard over the others. If you are viewed as someone with good money-making ideas, clients pay you back handsomely. Leader thrives on making sense out of the volatility, figuring out where the opportunities are and making those pay off for his clients.

Advice from Richard G. Leader. Before you can sell to clients, you have to learn how to sell, Leader says. The same principles apply everywhere. "Be genuinely interested in business and finance. You must be somewhat entrepreneurial and willing to take risks."

Path 5: Teaching

Many economists prefer to share their knowledge in the classroom rather than work in the field. Others, after a stint in government or the private sector, choose to finish their careers in an academic environment.

There are four main settings in which economics teachers usually work: secondary schools, community colleges, four-year colleges and universities, and adult-education programs.

1. Secondary schools: In many U.S. states and in Canada, economics is integrated throughout the curriculum from kindergarten through twelfth grade. Most school districts offer specific economics courses at the high school level.

2. Community colleges: Most community colleges offer courses in economics; some offer economics as a major for an associate's degree. Credits are usually transferable to a four-year college or university.

3. Four-year colleges and universities: The majority of economics courses are offered in four-year colleges and universities. Job positions range from instructors to full professors, with some programs hiring research assistants as well.

4. Adult-education programs: University evening and extension programs often offer economics as part of the curriculum. Instructors can be hired from the pool of day faculty or drawn from economists working in the field.

Responsibilities

In today's classrooms, economics teachers are using more props or sophisticated teaching aids, such as computers, DVDs, cameras, films, slides, and telecommunication systems, to help students understand abstract concepts, solve problems, and facilitate critical thinking.

Classes are becoming less structured, and students are working in groups to discuss and solve problems together. Preparing students for the future workforce is the major stimulus generating the changes in education. To be prepared, students must be able to interact with others, adapt to new technology, and logically think through problems. Teachers provide the tools and environment for their students to develop these skills.

Teachers observe and evaluate a student's performance and potential. Teachers increasingly are using new assessment methods, such as examining a portfolio of a student's graph work or writing, to measure student achievement. Teachers assess the portfolio at the end of a learning period to judge a student's overall progress. They may then provide additional assistance in areas where a student may need help.

Seeing students develop new skills and gain an appreciation of the joy of learning can be very rewarding. However, teaching may be frustrating when dealing with unmotivated and disrespectful students.

This is not usually the case at the college level, however. College students have demonstrated their dedication to academics and are generally receptive to ideas proposed in lectures and classes, even if they're taking economics as a required course.

College faculty usually spend fewer hours in the classroom than secondary school teachers do, but they have as many meetings, if not more. Often they are responsible for guiding students, at both undergraduate and graduate levels, supervising course selection, theses, and dissertation. Research and writing for scholarly journals is a large part of a university professor's routine, although this is less so at the community college level. Achieving substantial publications is usually a prerequisite for promotion, a professorship, and tenure.

Preparing for the Job

Aspiring secondary school teachers either major in the subject they plan to teach while also taking education courses, or major in education and take subject courses. Some states require a master's degree for permanent teacher certification.

More often than not, a Ph.D. is required for teaching at the college level, both at four-year and two-year colleges. However, some community colleges will hire instructors with master's degrees.

If you are interested in a career in college teaching but are concerned about the additional costs of graduate school, you shouldn't let that deter you. The vast majority of students in Ph.D. programs in economics receive assistant-ships or fellowships that cover the cost of tuition and provide an annual income of $8,000 to $12,000 per year.

Career Outlook

Secondary Schools

The job market for teachers varies widely by geographic area and by subject specialty. Many inner cities—characterized by high crime rates, high poverty rates, and overcrowded conditions—and rural areas—characterized by their remote location and relatively low salaries—have difficulty attracting enough teachers, so job openings should continue to be more frequent in these areas than in suburban districts.

Currently, many school districts have difficulty hiring qualified teachers in some subjects—economics, mathematics, science (especially chemistry and physics), bilingual education, and computer science. Specialties that currently have an abundance of qualified teachers include general elementary education, English, art, physical education, and social studies. Teachers who are geographically mobile and who obtain licensure in more than one subject should have a distinct advantage in finding a job.

With enrollments of minorities increasing, coupled with a shortage of minority teachers, efforts to recruit minority teachers should intensify. Also, the number of non-English-speaking students has grown dramatically, especially in California, Florida, Texas, and Arizona, which have large Spanish-speaking student populations, creating demand for bilingual teachers and those who teach English as a second language (ESL).

Overall employment of secondary school teachers is expected to increase about as fast as the average for all occupations through 2014. Demand will vary greatly. In areas with slow or negative population growth, such as the Northeast and upper Midwest, demand for teachers will grow more slowly than average or even decline. Western states, particularly California, Arizona, Nevada, Colorado, and Utah, will see much higher demand.

The number of teachers employed is also dependent on state and local expenditures for education. Pressures from taxpayers to limit spending could result in fewer teachers than projected; pressures to spend more to improve the quality of education could increase the teacher workforce.

The supply of teachers also is expected to increase in response to reports of improved job prospects, more teacher involvement in school policy, and greater public interest in education.

In recent years, the total number of bachelor's and master's degrees granted in education has steadily increased. In addition, more teachers will be drawn from a reserve pool of career changers, substitute teachers, and teachers completing alternative certification programs, relocating to different schools, and reentering the workforce.

Colleges and Universities

Employment of college and university faculty is expected to increase much faster than the average for all occupations through 2014 as enrollments in higher education increase, though many of these openings will be part-time. Additional openings will arise as faculty members retire. The exodus of retiring teachers that began in the late 1990s, those who were hired decades ago to educate baby boomers, will continue in the years to come. Most faculty members likely to retire are full-time tenured professors.

However, in an effort to cut costs, some institutions are expected to either leave these positions vacant or hire part-time, nontenured faculty as replacements. Prospective job applicants should be prepared to face keen competition for available jobs as growing numbers of Ph.D. graduates, including foreign-born graduates, vie for fewer full-time openings. As more Ph.D.s compete for openings, those who have a master's degree may find themselves squeezed out of consideration at universities, though they will find ample opportunity in community colleges and continuing-education programs, which will expand. College enrollment should rise 15 to 20 percent between 2002 and 2014.

In the past two decades, keen competition for faculty jobs forced some applicants to accept part-time or short-term academic appointments that offered little hope of tenure and forced others to seek nonacademic positions. This trend of hiring adjunct or part-time faculty will continue as colleges and universities attempt to remain competitive and reduce costs; many colleges face reduced state funding for higher education.

Public, two-year colleges employ a significantly higher number of part-time faculty as a percentage of their total staff than public four-year colleges and universities, but all institutions have increased their part-time hiring. With uncertainty over future funding, many colleges and universities are continuing to cut costs by eliminating some academic programs, increasing class size, and closely monitoring all expenses. They're also increasingly relying on graduate teaching assistants to accommodate burgeoning enrollments. Teaching assistants account for about 9 percent of all postsecondary teachers.

The nonacademic job market affects the employment of college instructors. Excellent job prospects in a field—for example, computer science or, say, economics—encourage more students to enroll, increasing faculty needs in that field. On the other hand, poor job prospects in a field, such as history in recent years, discourage students and reduce demand for faculty.

Salaries

Secondary Schools

According to the National Education Association (NEA), the estimated average salary for all public secondary school teachers in 2005 was $48,100 a year. Private school teachers generally earn less than public school teachers. The NEA report reveals that despite steady wage increases for public school teachers over the past twenty years, when adjusted for inflation, salaries increased by just 11 percent between 1985 and 2005. In 2005, for example, salaries rose by 2.3 percent, but inflation increased 3.1 percent. The result: Recruiting and retaining quality teachers is becoming more difficult than ever before.

One contributing factor, NEA researchers point out, is that younger teachers, who start at much lower salary levels, are replacing the teachers who began retiring in waves in the late 1990s. See nea.org/edstats/images/05rankings-update.pdf for a state-by-state breakdown of average teacher salaries.

Colleges and Universities

Earnings vary according to faculty rank and type of institution, geographic area, and field. According to a survey by the American Association of University Professors, salaries for full-time faculty average $68,505. By rank, the average for professors was $91,548; associate professors, $65,113; assistant professors, $54,571; instructors, $39,899; and lecturers, $45,647.

Faculty in four-year institutions earn higher salaries, on the average, than those in two-year schools. Average salaries for faculty in public institutions ($66,851) are generally lower than those for private independent schools ($79,342) but higher than those for religion-affiliated private institutions ($61,103).

In fields with high-paying nonacademic alternatives—notably medicine and law but also engineering, economics, and business, among others—earnings exceed these averages. In others, such as the humanities and education, they are lower.

Most faculty members have significant earnings in addition to their base salary, from consulting, teaching additional courses, research, writing for publication, or other employment, both during the academic year and during the summer.

Most college and university faculty enjoy some unique benefits, including access to campus facilities, tuition waivers for dependents, housing and travel allowances, and paid sabbatical leaves. Part-time faculty have fewer benefits than full-time faculty and usually do not receive health insurance, retirement benefits, or sabbatical leave.

Sample Job Ads

To get an idea of the kind of positions available, examine the sample teaching and research job announcements in Exhibits 10.1 through 10.3.

Exhibit 10.1
ECONOMICS ANNOUNCEMENT

Position: Economics Instructor
Institution: College, Department of Economics
Location: Southern California

Description: College is seeking a dynamic and engaging classroom instructor with a broad knowledge of economics, theory, and application. Our economics department is committed to the value of understanding economics in order to make sense of the political and social worlds in which we live. The successful candidate will be able to (1) Teach a broad spectrum of general education students, including economics and business majors; (2) Revitalize our economics program; (3) Review and revise course content and sequence where necessary; (4) Work with division chair to identify and coordinate talented and dedicated adjunct faculty; (5) Perform the typical instructor tasks: evaluate and counsel students; hold regular office hours; plan and organize instructional materials toward course objectives and learning outcomes; participate in campus shared governance process through service on division and campuswide committees; maintain class and examination schedules, grade and attendance records, and perform other related duties as assigned. Starting at $47,356–$62,191 annually, based on documented education and experience.

Exhibit 10.2
ADJUNCT FACULTY ANNOUNCEMENT

Position: Adjunct Economics Instructor
Institution: Online university

Description: You'll be challenged each day to help provide comprehensive, strategic solutions for our students. The bachelor's and master's of business administration programs are designed to help students advance in the workplace and allow them to specialize in a number of professional fields. Both programs require students to take courses in economics. The BBA program focuses on economics in a global environment while the MBA focuses on economics in management.

Our accredited university is a community of career-focused individuals who want to inspire and instill in others the value of a quality education and take pride in the faculty and the success of the students. All degree programs are taught through our online course-delivery system. We incorporate Flash technology and interactive multimedia applications to enable students and professors to interact in real-time via chat sessions, e-mail, and discussion boards.

Requirements: Adjunct faculty are expected to place a strong emphasis on student-centered learning. They must maintain and honor office and chat hours on a weekly basis and adhere to pre-existing course curriculum and assessment standards. They are also expected to know cutting-edge developments within the field.

- Master's degree in economics, terminal degree preferred
- Established instructional philosophy focusing on student success and retention
- 1–2 years of teaching experience, online teaching preferred
- Experience within the industry

Exhibit 10.3

TEACHING ANNOUNCEMENT

Position: Adjunct Faculty, Economics Reports
Institution: College
Location: San Francisco

Description: We offer master's, bachelor's, and associate's degree programs in technology, business, and management and are seeking an adjunct instructor to teach Economics 312, Principles of Economics. This course introduces basic concepts and issues in microeconomics, macroeconomics, and international trade. Microeconomics concepts, such as supply and demand and the theory of the firm, serve as foundations for analyzing macroeconomic issues. Macroeconomic topics include gross domestic product (GDP) and fiscal and monetary policy, as well as international topics such as trade and exchange rates. This course stresses analyzing and applying economic variables of real-world issues.

Requirements: Minimum master's degree in related field (Ph.D. preferred). Minimum 3 years' teaching experience or equivalent professional presentation/work experience preferred. Ability to work with diverse student population. Excellent written and verbal communication skills.

APPENDIX A

Professional Associations

Professional associations and societies can provide a wealth of information when it comes time to decide on a career path and search out job openings and related resources. Some associations publish their own newsletters to help you stay abreast of developments in the field. Others offer career counseling, salary surveys, job-placement services, and relevant links for further research. Most important, consulting with and joining such associations can put you in touch with people who are passionate about their work and know what it takes to succeed in a career in economics.

General

American Agricultural Economics Association (AAEA)
415 South Duff Ave., Suite C
Ames, IA 50010
aaea.org

American Economic Association (AEA)
2014 Broadway, Suite 305
Nashville, TN 37203
vanderbilt.edu/AEA/

Canadian Economics Association (CEA)
economics.ca

The Econometric Society
Department of Economics
New York University
269 Mercer St., Seventh Floor
New York, NY 10003
econometricsociety.org

National Economic Association (NEA)
ncat.edu/~neconasc/

Actuaries

American Academy of Actuaries
1100 Seventeenth St. NW, Seventh Floor
Washington, DC 20036
actuary.org

American Society of Pension Professionals & Actuaries
4245 North Fairfax Dr., Suite 750
Arlington, VA 22203
asppa.org

Casualty Actuarial Society
4350 North Fairfax Dr., Suite 250
Arlington, VA 22203
casact.org

Society of Actuaries
475 North Martingale Rd., Suite 600
Schaumburg, IL 60173
soa.org/ccm/content

Banking, Finance, and Investment

State bankers associations can furnish specific information about job opportunities in their states, or you can contact individual banks to inquire about job openings and to obtain more details about the activities, responsibilities, and preferred qualifications of tellers.

Information about financial management careers; tellers and such banking occupations as loan officers and loan counselors; training opportunities; and the banking industry is available from

American Bankers Association
1120 Connecticut Ave. NW
Washington, DC 20036
aba.com

Financial Management Association, International
College of Business Administration
University of South Florida
4202 East Fowler Ave., BSN 3331
Tampa, FL 33620
fma.org

For information about financial careers in business credit management; the Credit Business Associate, Credit Business Fellow, and Certified Credit Executive programs; and institutions offering graduate courses in credit and financial management, contact

National Association of Credit Management (NACM)
8840 Columbia 100 Pkwy
Columbia, MD 21045
nacm.org

For information about careers in treasury management, from entry level to chief financial officer, and the Certified Treasury Professional program, contact

Association for Financial Professionals
7315 Wisconsin Ave., Suite 600 West
Bethesda, MD 20814
afponline.org

For information about the Chartered Financial Analyst program, contact

CFA Institute
560 Ray C. Hunt Dr.
Charlottesville, VA 22903
cfainstitute.org

For information about financial management careers in the health care industry, contact

Healthcare Financial Management Association
Two Westbrook Corporate Center, Suite 700
Westchester, IL 60154
hfma.org

Information about job opportunities for securities sales representatives may be obtained from the personnel departments of individual securities firms.

For information about job opportunities for financial services sales representatives in various states, contact state bankers associations.

Business

National Association for Business Economics (NABE)
1233 Twentieth St. NW, #505
Washington, DC 20036
nabe.com

Education

The National Education Association (NEA) is the nation's largest professional employee organization, representing more than 2.7 million elementary and secondary school teachers, higher-education faculty, education support personnel, school administrators, retired educators, and students preparing to become teachers.

National Association of Economic Educators (NAEE)
http://ecedweb.unomaha.edu/naee.htm

National Council for Accreditation of Teacher Education
2010 Massachusetts Ave. NW, Suite 500
Washington, DC 20036
ncate.org

National Education Association
1201 Sixteenth St. NW
Washington, DC 20036
nea.org

The National Council for Accreditation of Teacher Education's website lists institutions with accredited teacher-education programs.

For information on voluntary teacher certification requirements, contact

National Board for Professional Teaching Standards
1525 Wilson Blvd. Suite 500
Arlington, VA 22209
nbpts.org

High School Teaching

Information on certification requirements and approved teacher training institutions is available from local school systems and state departments of education. For information on teachers unions and education-related issues, consult

American Association of Colleges for Teacher Education
1307 New York Ave. NW, Suite 300
Washington, DC 20005
aacte.org

National Association of Independent Schools
1620 L St. NW, Suite 1100
Washington, DC 20036
nais.org

American Federation of Teachers
555 New Jersey Ave. NW
Washington, DC 20001
aft.org

For information on college teaching careers, contact

American Association of University Professors
1012 Fourteenth St. NW, Suite 500
Washington, DC 20005
aaup.org

Government

Applicants for federal government jobs should go through the government's official jobs site, USAJobs (usajobs.opm.gov). See Chapter 10 for more information.

Health Care

American College of Healthcare Executives
One North Franklin St., Suite 1700
Chicago, IL 60606
ache.org

A list of approved undergraduate programs and accredited graduate academic programs in health administration is available from

Association of University Programs in Health Administration
2000 Fourteenth St. North, Suite 780
Arlington, VA 22201
aupha.org

For information about opportunities in long-term care administration, check

American College of Healthcare Executives
One North Franklin St., Suite 1700
Chicago, IL 60606
ache.org

For information about opportunities in medical group practices and ambulatory care management, check

Medical Group Management Association
104 Inverness Terr. East
Englewood, CO 80112
mgma.com

History

Economic History Association (EHA)
Department of Economics
500 El Camino Real
Santa Clara University
Santa Clara, CA 95053
eh.net/EHA

Human Resources

For information about careers in employee training and development, contact

American Society for Training and Development
1640 King St., Box 1443
Alexandria, VA 22313
astd.org/astd

For information about careers and certification in employee compensation and benefits, contact

WorldatWork
(United States)
14040 North Northsight Blvd.
Scottsdale, AZ 85260
worldatwork.org/
(Canada)
P.O. Box 4520
Postal Station A
Toronto, ON M5W 4M4
worldatwork.org/waw/canada

Information about careers and certification in employee benefits is available from

International Foundation of Employee Benefit Plans
18700 West Bluemound Rd.
Brookfield, WI 53045
ifebp.org

Information about careers in arbitration and other aspects of dispute resolution is available from

American Arbitration Association
335 Madison Ave., Tenth Floor
New York, NY 10017
adr.org

For information about academic programs in industrial relations, contact

Labor and Employment Relations Associations (LERA)
University of Illinois at Urbana-Champaign
121 Labor and Industrial Relations Building
504 East Armory Ave.
Champaign, IL 61820
lera.uiuc.edu

Information about personnel careers in the health care industry is available from

American Society for Healthcare Risk Management
Human Resources Administration
One North Franklin, St. Thirty-first Floor
Chicago, IL 60606
ashrm.org/ashrm/aboutus/aboutus.html

For information about personnel and labor relations careers in government, contact

International Association of Workforce Professionals
1801 Louisville Rd.
Frankfort, KY 40601
iawponline.org

Insurance

General information about an insurance underwriter career is available from the home offices of many life insurance and property-liability insurance companies. Information about the insurance business in general and the underwriting function in particular is available from

The American Institute for CPCU and Insurance Institute of America
720 Providence Rd.
P.O. Box 3016
Malvern, PA 19355
aicpcu.org

Law

American Law and Economics Association (ALEA)
P.O. Box 208245
New Haven, CT 06520
amlecon.org

Marketing and Sales

American Marketing Association
311 South Wacker Dr., Suite 5800
Chicago, IL 60606
marketingpower.com

Promotion Marketing Association, Inc.
257 Park Ave. South, Suite 1102
New York, NY 10010
pmalink.org

Sales & Marketing Executives International
P.O. Box 1390
Sumas, WA 98295
smei.org

Market Research

Council of American Survey Research Organizations
170 North Country Rd., Suite 4
Port Jefferson, NY 11777
casro.org

Marketing Research Association
110 National Dr., 2d Floor
Glastonbury, CT 06033
mra-net.org

Public Relations

Public Relations Society of America
33 Maiden Ln., 11th Floor
New York, NY 10038
prsa.org

Real Estate

American Real Estate and Urban Economics Association (AREUEA)
P.O. Box 9958
Richmond, VA 23228
areuea.org

Science

Economic Science Association (ESA)
econ.nyu.edu/dept/esa/

APPENDIX B

Web Resources

Bureau of Labor Statistics
bls.gov

CareerJournal.com (*Wall Street Journal*)
careerjournal.com

Chronicle of Higher Education
http://chronicle.com

Economics Jobs
economicsjobs.com

Economics Job Search
inomics.com/cgi/job

Freakonomics
freakonomics.com

The Internet Public Library
ipl.org/div/subject/browse/bus28.00.00/

Monster
http://content.monster.com/

AEA Web: Resources for Economics on the Internet
http://rfe.org/

Yahoo! HotJobs
http://hotjobs.yahoo.com/careertools

Index